Oxford Tube

AN ILLUSTRATED HISTORY
BY MALCOLM CROWE

CELEBRATING THE FIRST 25 YEARS

Presbus
PUBLISHING

First published 2012

ISBN 9780 9565 0614 6

Published by Presbus Publishing, PO Box 636, Portsmouth PO2 9XR
02392 655224
presbusps@btinternet.com

Design and layout: Rob Wilcockson

Printed in England by Ian Allan Printing Ltd, Hersham, Surrey, KT12 4RG

Front cover: Van Hool T827 Astromega Stagecoach in Oxfordshire 50213 (OU59 FNG) is seen at speed on the M40 near Beaconsfield, heading for London in January 2012. PHILIP LAMB

Back cover above: **Plaxton Paramount III 3500-bodied Volvo B10M No 22 (J456 FSH) makes its way along the M40 near Thame in 1999.**

Back cover below: **Seen leaving Oxford when new in 1996 is No 32 (M47 MJO), a Volvo B10M with Berkhof Excellence 1000LD coachwork.** Both: PHILIP LAMB

Previous page: **Van Hool T827 Astromega 50205 (T60 UBE) pulls away from Thornhill Park & Ride on the last leg of its journey from London, the last stop being Gloucester Green bus station in Oxford city centre.** PETER EDGAR

Contents

Acknowledgements

Thanks are due to many people who have provided assistance in the form of factual information, memorabilia, photographs etc, notably Martin Sutton (Managing Director, Stagecoach in Oxfordshire), Robert Williams (Commercial Manager, Stagecoach in Oxfordshire), Andrew Buckingham (driver examiner/ instructor, Stagecoach in Oxfordshire), Nick Clarke (Controller, Oxford Tube), Andy Johnson (Controller, Oxford Tube), Barry Pickett (Controller, Stagecoach in Oxfordshire), Joyce Pickett (former driver, Oxford Tube, Stagecoach in Oxfordshire), Dave Castle (former driver, Oxford Tube) and Richard Pimm (driver, Oxford Tube); also Ralph Adams, a long-term observer of all matters Oxford Tube and Gavin Francis, who has made available his extensive photographic collection.

Foreword

This book has been produced to celebrate the 25th anniversary of the Oxford Tube and traces the origins, background and development of a service which has become world-renowned as the way to travel between Oxford and London.

My early years were spent in the North West, living in Cheshire and learning about the industry and developments from publications such as *Bus & Coach* and *Buses Illustrated* (now *Buses*). These helped me to keep up with developments in most parts of the country. I also learned that new operators would find it difficult to start up and gain the licences required to maybe compete against the established operators.

Having passed my PSV test in 1961 and driven for Jacksons of Altrincham — later to become the nucleus of Shearings Holidays, then Melba Motors (part of North Western) and later Ribble Motor Services. I then embarked upon a career in the airline industry which lasted some 40 years.

During my time in the Midlands I drove part-time for Harpers of Heath Hayes, but a move to London in the mid-1970s focused

my interest on operations in Oxfordshire and Buckinghamshire and the changing face of the industry, with firstly the formation of the National Bus Company and in the 1980s the deregulation of bus and coach services, which brought about the introduction of a large number of new operators including in Oxford, Thames Transit.

As someone who had become used to the status quo, the idea of a new operator in Oxford, not only operating minibuses in the city, but also starting an express coach service to London against the established operator filled me with interest and a desire to understand how this could be.

So, how would this newcomer and its London service named the Oxford Tube, fare against the establishment? I started taking photographs and collecting timetables etc, and travelled on one of the early services boarding a Plaxton-bodied Leyland Tiger complete with host to serve me coffee or tea on my journey to London. The coach had a toilet, something the other company did not provide and fewer seats giving plenty of legroom.

I was most impressed and thought: 'One day I'm going to write a book about this', little realising that one day I would work for the company.

Today the Oxford Tube enjoys around 70% market share on the route. A tribute, to the far-sightedness of its founder Harry Blundred and all those who, over the years, have worked to make it an internationally known 24/7/365 operation.

Malcolm Crowe
Stokenchurch
February 2012

Left: **Van Hool T827 Astromega No 50202 on test at Thornhill Park & Ride prior to the type's entry into service in 2009.**
MALCOLM CROWE

Introduction

Top far right: **This Leyland Tiger TD4 with Scammell & Nephew 28-seat body was one of four similar vehicles delivered in 1931 to replace the charabancs used on the South Midland service since its inception. Seen here at Gloucester Green, No 29 (JO 1599) remained in service throughout the war years and beyond, finally being replaced by a Duple-bodied AEC Regal III.**
COURTESY PAUL LACEY

Below: **South Midland 17 (WL 7456) was an Arnold & Comben-bodied Dennis F new in 1928. It was a regular performer on South Midland's London service for almost 10 years.**
COURTESY PAUL LACEY

The coach service between Oxford and London, a distance of around 58.4 miles, has been an essential part of the Oxford public transport scene for many years. Established in 1921, it was operated initially by a small coach company called South Midland, established in Oxford by William Beasley, an ex-serviceman, running via Henley and Maidenhead. Beasley had already established his company in the excursion market, but this was a foray into the unknown. Using all-Dennis 2½-ton charabancs, this became a daily service, initially on a seasonal basis and by 1928 had become a regular service with state-of-the-art coaches picking up and setting down passengers *en route*.

But South Midland had competitors. By 1930 no fewer than 18 companies were running a total of 58 services between Oxford and London every day. As a result of the Road Traffic Act of 1930, the competitors were reduced to two, South Midland and Varsity Express, the latter having commenced operations the previous year. It is worth noting here that The City of Oxford Motor Services had operated a London service from 1921 but only on an intermittent basis until the General Strike of 1926, when it ceased altogether.

Varsity Express used a different route, using the A40, via High Wycombe and Uxbridge. Following interest from Black & White Motorways of Cheltenham in its Oxford route, from which a sale did not materialise, the Eastern Counties Omnibus Co acquired Varsity Express (which also ran a service between London and Cambridge in 1933. However, in 1934, Eastern Counties' parent, the Tilling Group, transferred the Oxford service of Varsity Express to United Counties, which with its headquarters in Northampton was a geographically more appropriate company within the group. In that year South Midland was

Above: **The Thames Valley era was typified by standard Bristol types, in particular LSs and MWs. This Bristol LS6G was new in 1952 as South Midland 83 (SFC 869) and spent many years on the London service. Here it waits outside the South Midland Café at Gloucester Green some time in the early 1960s.**
COURTESY PAUL LACEY

Above: **No 23 (LJB 423E), a 1967 Bristol RELH6G arrives in Oxford during the closing years of South Midland's tenure. This coach passed to the City of Oxford Motor Services on 1 January 1971, remaining on the service throughout the following decade.** PRESBUS ARCHIVE

operating seven journeys a day, whilst Varsity Express operated eight. The day return fare at this time was 6s (30p).

Beasley had also been seeking a buyer for South Midland, but with less success. In fact no buyer came forward at all as the 1930s progressed, and inevitably the outbreak of World War 2 had a profound effect on both Oxford–London operators, but the closing years of the war saw the sale of South Midland to Red & White Services of Chepstow, a company with which South Midland had established a working relationship over a decade previously.

In line with the postwar Labour Government's agenda, the Tilling Group, of which United Counties was a part, was nationalised in 1948, bringing the

one-time Varsity Express operations into state ownership. Two years later, fearing compulsory nationalisation, the Red & White group, which included in its portfolio United Welsh, Cheltenham District, Newbury & District and Venture of Basingstoke, sold out voluntarily to the British Transport Commission, and so following almost three decades of competition the two operators on the Oxford London services finally found themselves in common ownership.

Along with Newbury & District, control of South Midland passed immediately to the Thames Valley Traction Co, a BTC subsidiary based in Reading, but with an operating base in High Wycombe. However, it was not until 1 May 1952 that services on the Oxford–London corridor

Left: **In 1972/73 COMS took delivery of six Bristol RELH6Gs with ECW coach bodies primarily for use on the London services. These, plus three Plaxton Elite II-bodied REs, were the best vehicles available until the first of a new fleet of Leyland Leopards arrived in 1977.** RICHARD GOW

Below: **Oxford South Midland 80 (RBW 80L) was one of a number of dual-purpose Bristol RELH6Gs which also operated the 290 and 390 during the 1970s.** PRESBUS ARCHIVE

Above: **The late 1970s/early 1980s saw the arrival of the first of a number of better quality vehicles for the London services including COMS 104 (EBW 104Y), a Duple Dominant IV Express-bodied Leyland Tiger delivered in 1983. It is seen here at Victoria in the early years of deregulation in the blue and yellow livery introduced by NBC in 1983.** MALCOLM CROWE

were finally rationalised, following the BTC's decision to transfer the United Counties operation, including its garage and vehicles, to South Midland. The greatly enlarged South Midland company duly moved into the former United Counties premises in Botley Road, but overall control remained with Thames Valley, South Midland having previously occupied premises in Iffley Road, the remains of which can still be seen, now the home of a Peugeot dealer.

Throughout the 1950s and '60s South Midland exclusively operated both of the Oxford–London routes, non-stop coaches starting in 1963, reducing the journey time to 2hr 15min, as well as on its long-standing routes to Southsea

and to Worcester, its coaches adopting a pleasing non-standard maroon and cream livery which served to highlight its individuality among similarly styled liveries endemic within the BTC empire. A well-respected extended-tour programme with destinations including Ireland was also developed during the 1960s, but politics were about to intervene once again.

In 1968, under pressure from the then Labour Government, the privately owned British Electric Traction group sold its British bus-operating interests to the state, and this paved the way for the creation, under the terms of the Transport Act 1968, of the National Bus Company, which from 1 January 1969 assumed control of state-owned bus companies in England and Wales. Perhaps inevitably the new conglomerate sought to achieve economies where operations of the former BET and Tilling groups overlapped, and in line with this policy control of South Midland, along with its fleet of 33 coaches, passed on 1 January 1971 to the local former BET subsidiary, The City of Oxford Motor Services, the enlarged company trading henceforth as 'Oxford-South Midland'.

Under COMS auspices the Oxford–London express services were combined with COMS stage-carriage services along the same corridors, and as a result became pay-as-you-enter rather than pre-booked, becoming routes 30 (Oxford–Henley–London) and 70 (Oxford–High Wycombe–London), the numbers being changed in 1975 to 390 and 290 respectively.

The M40 motorway between London and Oxford opened in stages from 1967 to 1976. Occasional non-stop services used the motorway, but in 1977 a regular non-stop service was started as route 190, later renumbered X90.

In the 1980s a non-stop service, the X70, was introduced between Oxford and Heathrow Airport, whilst the 290 stopping service became a joint operation with Green Line, which at the time provided a service between London and High Wycombe. However, by this time far-reaching changes were afoot which were to have a profound effect upon the provision of bus and coach services in the UK as a whole and which were to lead to the creation of the subject of our story, The Oxford Tube.

Below: **The year 1985 saw the arrival of the first double-deck 'true' coaches on the Oxford-London service with the introduction by COMS of eight MCW Metroliners. These were also the first tri-axle coaches to run on the service.** MALCOLM CROWE

1. The birth of Thames Transit

By the end of the 1970s a radical overhaul of road-based public transport was being planned by the newly elected Conservative Government, and it was not long before these plans started to come to fruition. The Transport Act 1980 deregulated express coach services, and an early exponent of the new opportunities was British Coachways, a consortium of established operators including Grey-Green of London, Wallace Arnold of Leeds and Devon, Shearings of Altrincham, Park's of Hamilton, Morris Bros of Swansea and Ellerman-Bee Line of Middlesbrough, which set up a network of services to compete directly with National Express, the recognised market leader in the provision of express coach services in Britain.

The success of the 1980 Act, in terms of stimulating competition and thereby increasing the quality of services provided, prompted the Government

to turn its attention to buses, and the Transport Act 1985 dispensed with the licensing of local bus services in favour of deregulation (effective 26 October 1986), whereby operators were free to register services commercially. To encourage competition the 1985 Act also required NBC to be sold off piecemeal to the private sector.

Even before privatisation was mooted, changes were afoot in Oxford. In 1984, as part of an ongoing reorganisation among NBC's operating subsidiaries, 'Oxford-South Midland' was divided into two separate units; COMS retained the Oxford city services and the majority of the London expresses (though not the 390), while a new South Midland company assumed responsibility for what had hitherto been COMS's 'country' operations.

Enter Harry Blundred, who had worked for City of Oxford as Traffic Manager before being appointed General Manager of the newly created Devon General Ltd (another product of NBC's reorganisations) in 1983. Blundred believed that minibuses could revolutionise the bus operation by bringing low-cost, high frequency services to an industry that was performing well below its potential. In 1984 he established a pioneer operation in Exeter using Ford Transits with coachbuilt bodies on four routes resulting in a three-fold increase in passenger numbers by the end of the year. The Devon General management,

Below: **Oxford Minibus and Oxford Tube vehicles at Exeter in February 1987, being prepared for the launch in Oxford the following month.** THAMES TRANSIT

Right and below right:
Members of Thames Transit's opening fleet leave Belgrave Road, Exeter, for Oxford on 1 March 1987. The minibus is Ford Transit/ Mellor No 139, the coach Leyland Tiger/Duple No 7.
GRAHAM SELWAY

led by Blundred, soon made an offer to buy the company, and, having been approved by the Minister of Transport, the sale was completed on 19 August 1986 — the first involving an NBC bus operating subsidiary.

With developments in Devon well underway Blundred now turned his attention to other areas where his ideas he could work and, not unexpectedly, reasoned that Oxford would make a great place to establish a minibus-based operation. Thus was launched Thames Transit, initially with two routes. One used the prime corridor from the large Blackbird Leys housing estate into the city centre, on which it was felt, the minibus concept would work well; the other — a surprise at

the time — was that from Oxford to London in direct competition with the incumbent operator, City of Oxford, Blundred being of the opinion that he could not enter the bus market whilst ignoring the development potential of this inter-city service. Thus was conceived the 'Oxford Tube'.

During the latter part of 1986 a small team from Devon General took up residence in an Oxford hotel and set about recruiting staff for the fledgling Thames Transit company. Drivers were taken on for both routes, this at a time when an 18-year-old could drive a minibus, but full-size vehicles required drivers of 21 or over.

Work was in hand in Exeter to have everything ready for Saturday 7 March

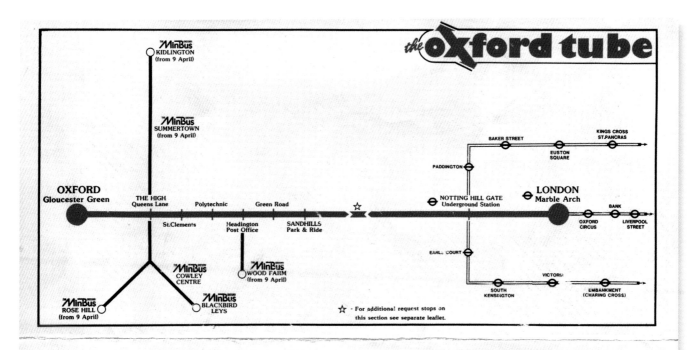

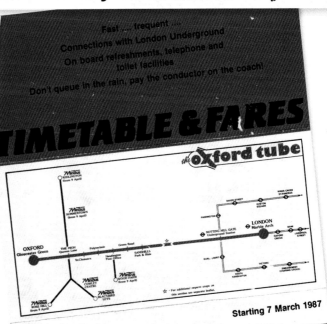

Timetable for the start of the Oxford Tube on Saturday 7 March 1987.

Above: **Leyland Tiger/Plaxton No 1 bound for London in the early days of the service.** IAN KIRBY

Below: **Tiger/Plaxton No 2 at Oxford's Gloucester Green bus station on layover between journeys from and to the capital. Its condition suggests the photograph was taken shortly after the service began.** IAN KIRBY

1987, the date set for the launch of the Oxford operations. The coaches were prepared at Devon General's workshops in Exeter, while the minibuses were delivered there by coachbuilder Mellor. The entire fleet was then moved to Oxford, where a depot, shared with a cement company whose business has been at this location for many years, was established at Horspath.

On the big day Blundred's team awoke to discover that heavy snow had fallen overnight. Not to be discouraged, Blundred took the first service out of Oxford to London himself, driving carefully in the difficult conditions but doubtless very proud of his one-time National Express coach, now resplendent in Oxford Tube's distinctive livery of red and grey.

On that first morning the service ran to Marble Arch, having departed Oxford

(Gloucester Green) at 06.35. Following a fast run on the M40 the coach dropped off at Notting Hill Gate (near the Underground station) at around 07.50 before reaching its destination at 07.55 — a journey time of 1hr 20min. The day-return fare was £2.97; a single was £2.90, and a period return £4.95. Stops on the way out of Oxford were High Street/Queen's Lane, St Clements, the Polytechnic (now Brookes University), Headington Post Office, Green Road and the Sandhills lay-by opposite Thornhill Park & Ride (the extended site, with its own bus station, was not brought into use until mid-2005). The stop at Lewknor was made on a 'request' basis, as were a number of others as the service struggled to its feet. An early stage chart referred to Lewknor turn, Beaconsfield turn and Uxbridge (canal lay-by)

Harry recalls that on the morning in question, before he left for the return journey scheduled at 08.05, he was interviewed live by BBC Oxford via the public phone fitted to the coach, this in the days before the widespread use of the mobile telephone. The interview eventually took place at 8.15, having been pushed back by the more dramatic news that morning concerning the *Herald of Free Enterprise* ferry disaster, which understandably took priority. Thus the 'Boss' went on to suffer the ignominy of arriving back in Oxford 10 minutes late.

The service required seven coaches, and eight were prepared initially. All were Leyland Tigers, two — Nos 1 and 2 (AOD 648/9Y) — with Plaxton Paramount 3200 bodies, and six — 3-8 (B400-3/5 UOD) — with Duple Laser 2 coachwork. All had been new to Devon General, running in the Greenslades fleet, and were four (Nos 1 and 2) or two years old (remainder). The 'missing' Tiger/Laser, B404 UOD, made occasional appearances to bolster the fleet but was not officially added to the Oxford Tube operation until November 1987, having previously been used in Oxford in National Express livery, when it received the fleet number 13.

Top: **Three of the Tiger/Duple coaches — from left to right Nos 6, 8 and 7 — in Exeter in February 1987, shortly before the Oxford Tube was launched.** DAVE GODLEY

Centre: **Duple Laser interior remained unchanged from National Express days, apart from the use of plain headrest covers.** RICHARD SHARMAN

Above: **A photograph taken in the early days of the service, featuring Tiger/Duple No 4 in London's Grosvenor Gardens.** GRAHAM SELWAY

Above: **November 1987 saw the final member of the batch of Leyland Tiger/Duple Laser coaches transferred from Devon. Still in National Express livery, with Greenslades subsidiary fleetnames and fleet number 2214, it is seen loading in George Street, where services terminated during the rebuilding of Gloucester Green bus station.**
MALCOLM CROWE

Right: **The first new coach for the fleet, delivered in July 1987, was a Leyland Tiger with Plaxton Paramount 3500 bodywork seating 51 and including a toilet, a standard feature on Tube coaches. It was numbered 9, its registration (D142 PTT) following on from the large batch of Ford Transit minibuses delivered earlier in the year for use on Thames Transit's Oxford Minibus network.**
MALCOLM CROWE

Left: **A trio of South Midland Carlyle-bodied Ford Transits shortly after being taken over by Thames Transit.** MALCOLM CROWE

Below: **Tiger/Duple No 4, by now named Brasenose, departs Gloucester Green on 9 November 1989, at which time the service was still using route number 100. Some dispute arose over the naming of coaches, colleges apparently expecting payment for being recognised In this way, and after two attempts the practice was abandoned.**
MALCOLM CROWE

Above: **Thames Transit's takeover of South Midland brought eight coaches, among them a pair of Leyland Tigers with Plaxton Paramount 3500 bodywork. Despite lacking washroom facilities they proved useful acquisitions; following withdrawal from passenger service in 1994 they would see further use as driver-training vehicles, as seen in this view of No 10 at Horspath early in 1995.**
MALCOLM CROWE

The key to the success of the service was the provision of 44 or 46 reclining seats, allowing greater legroom than on competing services, plus a refreshment service offering tea, coffee, biscuits etc, requiring the provision of a host/hostess on each coach. Initially a payphone was located by the washroom on each coach, but at that time technology was insufficiently far advanced for the system to work properly, and the phones were soon removed. Refreshments were not offered on late-evening departures, and the coffee machines would be withdrawn altogether by 1990.

Unfortunately loadings in the early days suggested that there were problems beyond malfunctioning telephones, so Harry's wife, Janet, undertook to go to Oxford to sort things out. Travelling on the service herself, she got to know the passengers and was able to establish what was wrong. Some adverse reaction was received regarding the host/hostess service, in particular the calibre of some of the

individuals employed. Subsequently Mrs Blundred appeared on local television, admitting that management had initially been lax and announcing that the employment of host/hostesses had ceased. It was also discovered that, if there were no passengers on board by Thornhill, it was not unknown for the driver to pull into a lay-by for a couple of hours and then return to Oxford at the expected time, but from then on steps were taken to ensure all coaches went all the way to London. Revenue started to improve almost immediately.

July 1987 saw the arrival of the first brand-new coach, purchased to permit extension of the service from Marble Arch to Victoria. A Plaxton Paramount III 3500-bodied Leyland Tiger, No 9 (D142 PTT) had 51 seats — a useful increase in capacity over that of the original coaches, albeit at the expense of legroom.

By the end of the first year of operation in March 1988 the future of the service was assured. Frequencies were increased from every 30min to

Above: **Further Tigers received from South Midland were a pair of Duple-bodied examples that had begun life with City of Oxford. Later to become No 13 in the Oxford Tube fleet, South Midland 126 (EBW 102Y) is seen at Wantage in 1987.** MALCOLM CROWE

Below: **Like the Plaxton-bodied pair, the two Duples were devoid of washroom facilities and could most often be found running between Oxford and Bicester, as demonstrated here by No 12 at Gloucester Green.** MALCOLM CROWE

Above: **Also acquired by Thames Transit from South Midland were four Leyland Leopards with ECW B51 bodywork. They were mostly to be found on the Bicester services, No 921 being thus employed when photographed at Gloucester Green in November 1989.**
MALCOLM CROWE

every 20min, the journey time to Victoria set at 100min and the service increased to 37 round trips per day. Highlights, besides the increased number of journeys were, extra Sunday journeys at 07.40 from Oxford and an return journey from London at 09.20. The day return fare remained the same to Marble Arch and intermediate stops but the fare to Victoria was set at £3.95 for a day return. £3.50 single, and a period return of £5.95. A one-week ticket for unlimited journeys cost just £13.99, whilst a one-year season ticket costing £495 was offered from 7 March 1988 and weekly, two-weekly, four-weekly and 13-weekly tickets were introduced. Season tickets could even be purchased from Post Offices in the Oxford area, whilst an Oxford Tube Travel club for an investment of just £5, offered cheaper travel with some journeys free of charge.

Further newer and more luxurious coaches were introduced and thee

was an extension of the service to Victoria, Marble Arch requiring a long walk in the evening. The new terminus at Grosvenor Gardens was most conveniently located for the train, bus and underground stations, but Victoria Coach Station was quite a walk away, especially if one has suitcases. At that time there were 28 services a day with the last coach leaving London at 00.05, arriving in Oxford at 01.15.

Passenger numbers rose steadily but there was no time to sit back and take it easy. The remainder of 1988 and 1989 were marked by an increase in the number of coaches in the fleet with a timetable now providing 42 departures on weekdays, 41 on Saturdays and 32 on Sunday from each end of the route.

Having left their Horspath base most Oxford Tube coaches entered service immediately on service 1A from the 'Original Swan' public house, picking up passengers on the Cowley Road into town prior to taking up duty on the London service, often also returning as a 1A. Another example of efforts to reduce dead mileage is provided by the working of car 'M', which left Horspath at 06.55 for Carterton, whence it departed at 07.35, calling at Queen Street, Oxford, at 08.40 before continuing to Gloucester Green for a connection to London.

Whilst local buses were allowed to use Cornmarket the Oxford Tube was not, Gloucester Green being reached instead via Speedwell Street. However, on at least one occasion an Oxford Tube coach was observed in Cornmarket masquerading as a 390 (which route was permitted to use the thoroughfare), its driver presumably anxious to save a few minutes!

Thames Transit had been expanding rapidly and had become a major force both on the streets of Oxford and across the wider area. In both domains it challenged the recently recreated South Midland company, which had been sold to its management on 19 December 1986. Ahead of sale by NBC this company had been allocated a fleet of 24 Ford Transits with parcel-van bodies converted into 16-seater minibuses by Carlyle in Birmingham in

Below: **In 1989 a third competitor appeared on the Oxford–London route in the form of National Express, Galloway of Mendlesham, Suffolk, using this Plaxton-bodied DAF SB2300 for the new 882 'London Express' service between Burford and the capital.**
MALCOLM CROWE

Above: **Acquired in 1989, and becoming No 15 this Plaxton Paramount 1-bodied Leyland Tiger had previously been engaged on National Express duties with Southern National as its SN2. It is seen here in Taunton early summer 1989 bound for Hull.** IAN TROTTER

Far right: **The same coach at Horspath on 18 December 1995.** MALCOLM CROWE

addition to three existing examples, allowing it to compete to some extent on the busy streets of Oxford itself. However, it proved to be something of a sickly child and was soon run out of town, its services being taken over by Thames Transit in 1989, making it an early casualty of the deregulation and privatisation process.

As a result of the takeover four former South Midland coaches — all of them Leyland Tigers — were transferred to the Oxford Tube. Nos 10 and 11 (C128/9 KJO) were fitted with 53-seat Plaxton Paramount II 3500 coachwork but were devoid of toilet facilities. Ordered by Yelloway, they had found their way into the South Midland fleet in July 1986; they would later be re-registered PYV 277 and LSV 670 respectively. The other pair comprised the first two 12m Duple Dominant IV-bodied Leyland Tigers (EBW 101/2Y) of a batch of 10 that

had been placed in service by COMS in 1983 in an attempt to improve the quality of the rolling stock on the London services, the pair passing to South Midland in 1984 when COMS was split. Also lacking toilets, these 50-seaters, numbered 12 and 13, were rarely used on the London services

Also acquired with the South Midland business were ex-COMS ECW B51-bodied Leyland Leopards VUD 28-30/2X, all four joining the main Thames Transit fleet. They had an interesting history thereafter, two spending the winter of 1989/90 in Devon, on loan to Brixham Coaches. As far is known the Leopards were never used on Oxford Tube's direct London service, although they may have been used on the 390.

By the spring of 1989 the fleet of coaches normally used on the service had reached a total of 12, sufficient to cover a peak vehicle requirement of 11. Coaches made three or four journeys per day, depending upon the duty to which they were allocated. Some repaint work was undertaken in 1989, and at around this time the early coaches were named after Oxford colleges. The practice was destined to be short-lived, however, as by 1990 the practice had stopped as it had been suggested that the colleges wanted payment for the use of their names.

During the early years competition between Thames Transit and COMS was intense, and there were some disagreements between the staff of the two companies. However, it should not be overlooked that at this time there was another competitor on the route. This was none other than National Express, which ran the London Express for a period of time. This service ran twice a day during the summer of 1989 and was routed from Burford via Eynsham, Witney, Minster Lovell,

Botley, Oxford (Gloucester Green and Sandhills to London Victoria. The regular vehicle, owned by Galloway of Mendlesham, Suffolk, was F764 RRT, a DAF SB2300 with 53-seat Plaxton Paramount III bodywork in full National Express livery, but using green instead of blue and 'London' in place of the word 'National'. However, although the concept appeared sound the service was not a success and was soon withdrawn.

The end of the 1980s saw the Oxford Tube well established, with a strong level of passenger support. The fleet numbered 15 vehicles, the most recent addition being No 15 (C922 HYA), a Plaxton Paramount II 3500-bodied Leyland Tiger acquired from Southern National. The early problems had all been resolved, and the company was poised to enter the 1990s and a further period of development

2. The 1990s and rapid development

The new decade began with the purchase of many new coaches, heralding a period of expansion. First to arrive, in October 1990, was a Volvo B10M-60, No 18 (H69 CFJ), fitted with a 51-seat Plaxton Paramount III 3200 body which included a washroom. In the same month two second-hand Leyland Tigers — the last to be acquired — arrived from Southern National. Numbered 16/7 (B896/4 YYD), they had 48-seat Paramount II 3200 bodywork, also with washroom facilities.

Thames Transit's acquisition of South Midland in 1989 had brought with it the 390 route, which, it will be recalled, was in effect the original South Midland service launched in 1921 save that the current version operated via Abingdon. From 1990 it ran as an Oxford Tube, with nine return journeys (plus one commuter express) on weekdays, and five on Saturdays and

Sundays. Also at this time a new service (400) was introduced from Abingdon to Aldgate in the City of London, serving Burcot, Dorchester, Wallingford, Henley and Maidenhead (Thicket Corner) *en route*. By March 1991 a revised timetable for the motorway service listed some 43 departures on weekdays, the earliest being 05.45 and the last at 22.30, with slightly fewer on Saturdays and Sundays.

The next new coaches, which were delivered in May 1991, were five Volvo B10M-60s with impressive Ikarus Blue Danube coachwork seating 49 and with the now standard washroom facility. These coaches took fleet numbers 19-23 and, like all new vehicles delivered thus far, were registered in Devon, as H913-7 HTT. The author took a trip to London on one of these coaches when it was almost brand-new and recalls being impressed by both the ride and the skilful handling of the vehicle, driven by a youthful Nick Clarke — now a controller at Gloucester Green. A sixth Volvo/Ikarus, No 24 (J499 MOD), joined the fleet in October.

In March 1992 the number of weekday return journeys rose to 47 and by October 1992 had reached 50. The service by then was every 20 minutes commencing 05.10 on weekdays.

April 1992 saw the arrival of more Ikarus-bodied Volvos in the shape of four nearly new examples from Hills of Tredegar, new examples of this chassis/ body combination being no longer available. They were numbered 25-8 (H914-7 PTG) and were less than a year old when acquired. Eagled-eyed readers will no doubt have spotted that their registrations closely replicated those of the previous year's new deliveries, which must have caused moments of confusion at allocation times.

Below: **Photographed shortly after entering service in October 1990, Volvo B10M/Plaxton Paramount No 18 was the second new coach acquired for the Oxford Tube, and the first of many Volvos.**
MALCOLM CROWE

390
OXFORD
Abingdon
Wallingford
Henley - on - Thames
Maidenhead
Heathrow
LONDON

OXFORD - LONDON EXPRESS
TEL: (0865) 772250

the oxford tube
OXFORD - LONDON
EVERY 20 MINS
IT'S A
WONDERFUL
WAY TO TRAVEL

B894 YYD

By now four of the Duple Laser-bodied Tigers had left the fleet, only Nos 4, 7, 8 and 14 (B401/5/6/4 UOD) remaining in service. In the spring of 1993 a final three Ikarus-bodied Volvos were taken on strength. Nos 29-31 (F23/4 LBW, F337 CHE) had operated previously with McLean's of Witney and for four-year-old coaches were still in very good condition internally.

The new timetable commencing 4 April 1993 showed the biggest changes in six years, for the first time offering overnight journeys These were to depart hourly from Oxford commencing at 23.15 and continuing until 04.15. From 05.10 there would be a departure every 20min throughout the day. Now there was truly no such thing as a last coach!

In August 1993 the first of a new combination appeared with the delivery of five Jonckheere Deauville 45-bodied Volvo B10M-62s. They were followed by a further pair in January 1994 and another five in April 1994. The 12 coaches were numbered 1-7, 18, 21/9-31 (L723/4 JUD, L210-4 GJO, L155/9/6-8 LBW), most taking fleet numbers vacated by earlier coaches by now withdrawn, including some only recently acquired. The sizeable intake of new coaches at this time meant that almost 40% of the Oxford Tube fleet was less than a year old.

Above: **More second-hand coaches arrived in the spring of 1990, when Southern National supplied a pair of Leyland Tigers with Plaxton Paramount 3200 bodywork seating 48. This picture shows No 17 on a 390 working in Bulleid Way, London, in July 1993.**
MALCOLM CROWE

The next coaches to arrive were four Plaxton Paramount 3500-bodied Volvo B10Ms. Taking vacant fleet Nos 10/1/5/7 (H639-41/50 UWR), these 48-seaters (with toilet) came from Wallace Arnold and were acquired specifically to upgrade the 390 service.

By now the Abingdon service was running as the 390 only (the number 400 having been dropped), comprising an 04.45 journey to Heathrow only, an 05.50 from Oxford to the City which continued to Victoria and six subsequent journeys, the last leaving Oxford at 17.45.

Left: **Duple Laser II-bodied Leyland Tiger No 4 soon outbound on the 390 and with Green Line Associated Service sticker waits at Gloucester Green alongside Volvo B10M/Ikarus Blue Danube No 21 (H915 FTT) allocated that day to the London (100) service.**
RICHARD SHARMAN

There were seven journeys on Saturdays, Sundays and Bank Holidays.

Early in 1994 the 390 was rebranded as 'The Heathrow Tube', becoming a 24hr service, with departures from Gloucester Green hourly from 06.15 and at 15min past each odd hour throughout the night. The new timetable meant that there were now 17 journeys per day to Heathrow and 19 journeys back, Saturdays and Sundays included. A day return fare of £6.00 to Heathrow applied. There was also an early-morning commuter run to the City (effectively a revival of the old 400), plus an equivalent return journey during the evening peak.

As might be imagined, the introduction of the improved service did not please the other operator on the route, City of Oxford. Whilst the 390 had always travelled via Heathrow it had not been promoted as such and had been regarded more as a pleasant way to travel from Oxford to London along the Thames Valley. Equally it provided a useful link for residents of those riverside towns wanting to spend a day in London or Oxford. The Heathrow Tube lasted about a year, and, following its demise

the 390 reappeared serving Heathrow via Wallingford, Henley and Maidenhead. The coaches branded for the Heathrow tube lost their branding and were used instead on the London direct service.

In March 1994 City of Oxford was sold by its management to Go-Ahead Group, and there followed a period of intense competition, COMS slashing its fares in an effort to bring down the 'upstart' Thames Transit, which was probably being rather too successful for its liking. Eventually, however, a change of management at COMS brought about a period of calm, which benefited bus and coach users in Oxford and thus ensured the long-term viability of both companies.

In the meantime 1994 also saw the increase in Oxford Tube frequency on the motorway route to every 10min at peak times, a level still being sustained in the winter of 1995/6. Also at this time the night schedule was hourly between 01.10

Below: **Between February 1992 and March 1993 seven more nearly new Volvo/Ikarus coaches joined the fleet — four from Hill's of Tredegar and three from McLean's of Witney. Among the latter was No 31, which arrived in March 1993 and was recorded three months later.** MALCOLM CROWE

Above: **New to McLean's of Witney in 1989, Volvo B10M/Ikarus 30 was one of three such vehicles which joined the Oxford Tube fleet in March 1993, being seen here early the following year at the Grosvenor Gardens terminus in London.** RICHARD SHARMAN

Left: **Leyland Tiger/Duple Laser II No 4 was withdrawn in 1993. It is seen here with subsequent owner Bearwood Coaches in the West Midlands.**
RICHARD SHARMAN

Below: **Jonckheere Deauville-bodied Volvo B10M 31 (L158 LBW) leaves Gloucester Green with a light load in 1995.**
PHILIP LAMB

Above: **Acquired in the autumn of 1994 to upgrade the 390 service were four Plaxton Paramount 3500-bodied Volvo B10Ms that had started life as tour coaches with Wallace Arnold. No 11 is seen at Hyde Park Corner in an interim livery used prior to the re-branding of this service as the Heathrow Tube.** M. PENN

Right: **Tried on the 390 by Thames Transit prior to the acquisition of the Plaxton-bodied Volvos was this Dennis Dart/ Wadham Stringer demonstrator, L766 DPE, pictured in November 1993.** RICHARD SHARMAN

Left: **The Oxford Tube service was publicised by the use of its livery on members of Thames Transit's Oxford Minibus fleet, including Mercedes-Benz 709D/ Reeve-Burgess 321, seen here in New Road.** RICHARD SHARMAN

Below: **No 15, another of the four ex-Wallace Arnold Plaxton-bodied Volvo B10Ms acquired in March 1994, at Gloucester Green in later red and grey with branding for the Heathrow Tube.** MALCOLM CROWE

and 04.10 from Oxford (and remains so to this day), the night service proving very popular with students, theatregoers and international travellers alike.

Thus by 1996 there were 83 round-trips per day on weekdays, a near-equal number on Saturdays but with a morning peak on the 10min service from 09.10 until 11.30. On Sundays the 10min peak service also operated in the late afternoon in both directions, meeting the needs of a travelling public who wanted capacity at the end of their weekend, whether in Oxford or London.

On the vehicle front, another five Volvo B10M-62s — Nos 9, 16, 25/6/8 (M103-7 XBW) — arrived in April 1995, this time with Berkhof Excellence 1000LD coachwork; they were followed in April 1996 by seven similar vehicles — 8, 12/4/9, 23, 32/3 (N41-3/5-8 MJO) — which proved to be the last new coaches purchased under the Transit Holdings regime. Interestingly, whilst these vehicles again took fleet numbers vacated by withdrawals, the number 13 remained unused after December 1991.

A survey of the fleet at the end of 1996 reveals 24 coaches delivered new since

August 1993 plus the four former Wallace Arnold coaches, whilst still in use were three of the Ikarus-bodied Volvos, by now five years old.

Fares from Oxford to Victoria were now £6.20 single, £6.50 day return and £8.50 period return; in 1987, when the service started, these had been £2.97, £2.90 and £4.95 respectively. In addition, equivalent student fares of £5.70, £6.00 and £6.50 were now on offer. Competition remained strong, COMS offering the same level of fares and operating 73 round-trips each weekday, although at this time it was not operating 24 hours a day, its earliest journeys not departing until 04.40, and the last at 00.15.

In 1997 Oxford Tube's London timetable offered 81 return services every weekday, 82 on Saturdays and 73 on Sundays. The service operated 364 days of the year and continuously throughout the night. The day-return fare had gone up to £7.00; a single was now £6.70 and a period return £9.00. Student fares were £6.00, £5.70 and £6.50 respectively — these fares also applied to children and senior citizens. A 'Tube 12' (12 single journeys with a validity of one year) cost £36, giving a return-trip equivalent of just £6.00. A weekly ticket was now £25, a two-week ticket £47, a four-week ticket £90, a 13-week ticket £280, and the price of an annual season ticket £700. These tickets also gave unlimited travel on Thames Transit buses in its zones 1 and 2. A Gold Card was available giving unlimited travel on the Oxford Tube and all Thames Transit bus services for two years at a cost of £1,350. Another innovation was the 'Londoner' — a through ticket from the holder's nearest local bus stop to London via Thames Transit and the Oxford Tube.

Above: **No 14 (N42 NJO), a Berkhof Excellence 1000LD-bodied Volvo B10M is seen in Worcester Street Oxford at the start of its 90min run to Victoria.** PHIIP LAMB

Top far left: **Displaying the gold livery introduced to mark the 10th anniversary of the Oxford Tube in 1997 is coach No 8 (N41 MJO), a Berkhof Excellence-bodied Volvo B10M.** MALCOLM CROWE

Bottom far left: **A challenge for passengers! Can you find the '21'?** RICHARD SHARMAN

Right: **The Heathrow Tube coaches were later transferred to the London service upon cessation of the former. Here at Horspath No 10 (H639 UWR) displays its own distinctive variation of the anniversary livery.** MALCOLM CROWE

The journey time was scheduled at 90min, but a comment on the timetable warned passengers to allow longer at busy times. In 1987 the company had offered nearly 1,400 seats per day, but by 1997 had risen to just over 4,000 seats per day, a remarkable increase in just 10 years. The sustained growth of the company in the face of the competition from COMS meant that passengers were offered an unrivalled service between the capital and a major seat of learning, the like of which has never been bettered anywhere in the world. The coaches were in the main the latest the industry could offer, all being equipped with washroom facilities — unusual on short-distance express services, the mileage for the journey being just under 60 miles each way. Moreover, schedules now demanded that vehicles cover some 3.5 million miles per year, compared to just over 1 million miles 10 years previously. That all this was accomplished by a start-up company plying against an established competitor was no mean feat and provides a rare example of what the deregulation of the industry had set out to achieve.

The livery had changed somewhat, and although red and grey were still the basic colours the fleetname displayed on the coaches had been updated, now consisting of a shaded blue oblong with '**oxford tube**' running through. It was felt, however, that something special was called for to celebrate the 10th anniversary, and so a revised livery was introduced which featured red and gold as the base colours. Volvo/Berkhof No 12 further had its fleet number repeated all along the skirt panels, a challenge being to find the '21' deliberately inserted to test the public's observational skills!

Interestingly, whilst Oxford Tube was celebrating its 10th anniversary COMS was claiming 70 years of linking Oxford with London. The latter claim was somewhat dubious, however, COMS having run on only an intermittent basis until the General Strike of 1926 and thereafter leaving the field clear until 1971, when it assumed control of South Midland; given Thames Transit's takeover in 1989 of the 'new' South Midland (which, incidentally, would not finally be wound up until 1998) it is open to interpretation as to which has the stronger claim to being the oldest operator on the route …

3. Stagecoach takes over

As a result of Thames Transit continuing to grow and prosper, interest amongst the big players in the bus industry was attracted, and as a result it was purchased by Stagecoach Holdings PLC in July 1997, bringing the Oxford Tube into that group's portfolio.

At Stagecoach development and modernisation is always to the forefront. This had also been the case in Thames Transit's independent days, but following the takeover time was taken to consider replacements for the existing coach fleet.

The oldest coaches among the 32 then in use were the four 1991 Volvos acquired second-hand from Wallace Arnold for use on the Heathrow Tube, the remainder dating from between 1993 and 1996. At this time annual passenger loadings were around 1.5 million, and during busy periods weekly totals sometimes exceeded 30,000. Loadings clearly dictated larger coaches, but of which type?

It seemed that the answer might just be found within the wider Stagecoach fleet. In 1996 it had placed in service a number of

Below: **In standard Oxford Tube livery, ex Wallace Arnold Volvo B10M/ Plaxton Paramount III 3500 (H650 UWR), Oxford Tube 17 departs Oxford for London in November 1995.**
PHILIP LAMB

72-seat articulated Volvo coaches — might these be the answer for extra capacity on the Oxford Tube? A trial was held as early as August 1997, demonstrating how quickly the new owner could make things happen. The coach chosen was a year-old Volvo B10MA-55 with Jonckheere Modulo coachwork, numbered 561 (N561 SJF) in the Fife Scottish fleet. Lettered 'Stagecoach Express' and branded for the X27 (Glasgow–Cumbernauld–Dunfermline–Kirkcaldy–Leven–Anstruther) service, it made a fine sight on the Oxford–London route. But it was not all plain sailing: one driver, attempting to turn around at Gloucester Green, managed to get the coach jack-knifed, causing mayhem, and thereafter it was barred from Gloucester Green, using George Street as its terminus. One may safely assume that such incidents weighed heavily upon the management of the time, and orders for such coaches for the Oxford Tube were not forthcoming.

As it transpired, we would have to wait two years to discover how Stagecoach was going to increase seating capacity on the service. As a result there followed a period of consolidation under the

new management, and in the latter half of 1997 a number of extra coaches were acquired as a stopgap measure. Stagecoach Midland Red provided two Plaxton Paramount 3500-bodied Volvo B10Ms (with 'dateless' registrations 3063 VC and 9258 VC) which took fleet numbers 3 and 6. Received at around the same time were four more B10Ms. One, No

Above: **No 22 retained its National Express moquette — a somewhat awkward marriage to the Oxford Tube antimacassars!** MALCOLM CROWE

Top far left: **Stagecoach Fife articulated Volvo B10M/ Jonckheere 561 being trialled in Oxford Tube service in George Street, Oxford, in August 1997.** MALCOLM CROWE

Bottom far left: **The pair of former Stagecoach Midland Red Plaxton Paramount III-bodied Volvo B10Ms taken into stock in 1997 initially retained their Midland Red coach livery, which as can be seen did not look that out of place. No 3 (3063 VC) is seen here at Hyde Park Corner shortly after entering service. This coach had been new to Wallace Arnold as G543 LWU in 1990.** M. PENN

Left: **Acquired the previous year from Stagecoach Midland Red, Volvo B10M/ Plaxton Expressliner No 22 looked very smart when photographed in the new red-and-gold livery on 4 April 1998.** RICHARD SHARMAN

Above: **No 20 (J420 HDS)** was one of a pair of Plaxton Excalibur-bodied B10Ms which entered service in 1997. Both had previously been with Stagecoach Busways in Flightlink livery, but were new to Park's of Hamilton. The coach is seen here in Woodstock in 1998 on X50 duties.
MALCOLM CROWE

Right: **Upon arrival this loaned Leyland Tiger carried the mark 9737 VC, but reverted to its original registration C212 PPE before return. Originally London Country STL12, it had arrived from Stagecoach Midland Red, where it carried fleet No 75.**
MALCOLM CROWE

Above: **The only Plaxton Premiere-bodied coach to run on the Oxford Tube is P186 NAK, a Volvo B10M hired in during 1997/98. It had been new to Kilpatrick of Glenrothes, Fife.**
MALCOLM CROWE

22 (J456 FSR), also ex-Stagecoach Midland Red but new to Express Travel Services, Perth, in 1992, had a Plaxton Expressliner body (based on the Paramount 3500) and had been built specifically for National Express work; indeed, it still had National Express moquette covering its seats, which looked incongruous when fitted with Oxford Tube antimacassars. However, it gained full livery of red and gold, as did the other two arrivals. These were the first coaches in the fleet with Plaxton Excalibur coachwork and looked superb in their new colours. Numbered 20/4 (J420/4 HDS), they seated 44 (with toilet) so offered generous legroom. New to Park's of Hamilton, Nos 20/4 had come via Stagecoach Busways. Although older than the coaches employed on Oxford Tube work, these Volvos had been worked much less hard, and their acquisition permitted the withdrawal of five of the L-registered Jonckheere-bodied B10Ms, which were becoming rather careworn.

In 1998 additional coaches appeared on loan to provide extra capacity, among them two low-driving-position Leyland Tigers with Plaxton Paramount 3500 coachwork from Stagecoach Midland Red. Both were 51-seaters and fitted with toilets. Registered 4828 VC and 9737 VC, they had started life with London Country in 1985 as its STL11/2 (C211/2 PPE). These coaches did not gain Oxford Tube livery but ran with small notices in the front window proclaiming 'extra coach'. Two other loaned coaches ran in overall white, these being Volvo B10M/Plaxton Première 3500 P186 NAK, new to Kilpatrick of Glenrothes, Fife, and B10M/ Caetano Algarve II M332 GFW, new to Dalsy of Broughton, Lincolnshire.

At the end of 1998 the fleet strength remained fairly steady, but with the short-term addition of the four loaned coaches described above. One point of interest is that most of the coach fleet

This page: **What lurks beneath? The launch of the new MAN 24.350/Jonckheere Monaco double-decker coaches was a lavish affair. Here, surrounded by dry ice and accompanied by a pair of pretty girls, No 36 is revealed to the assembled throng.** MALCOLM CROWE

at this time had conventional manual gearboxes, the Tigers having had hydracyclic transmission.

On the service side, stops at Lewknor and Hillingdon had been formalised, and the route had settled into a period of stability, still with a journey time of around 90min but with extra capacity urgently required, as support from the travelling public continued to increase.

The year 1999 started inauspiciously, with a fleet of varied types and colours, although red-and-gold seemed to predominate for a while. Rumours of a new fleet abounded, but all concerned both at the company and elsewhere remained tight-lipped. Come February, however, the secret was out, and it was learned that a fleet of double-deck coaches was due take to the road in the spring.

On Saturday 5 April one of the new coaches, an MAN 24.350 with Jonckheere Monaco bodywork, was used to launch a new era in Oxford Tube travel. The 68-seat double-decker coach with dual doors was fitted with a toilet and refreshment facilities on the lower deck. The coach was also wheelchair-accessible. The new fleet took numbers 34-60 (T34-6 DFC, T37-9 BBW, T40 UBE, T41-3 BBW, T44 UBE, T45-9 BBW, T50 UBE, T51-4 BBW, T55 UBE, T56-9 BBW and T60 UBE) — a total of 27 vehicles. The use of personalised registrations for some of the fleet was interesting, but one wonders why

Left and below:
Monaco interior followed standard Stagecoach practice at the time.
MALCOLM CROWE

Above left: **No 53 (T53 BBW) was one of eight coaches specifically equipped to accommodate a wheelchair.**
MALCOLM CROWE

they were not applied to every coach. First to arrive was No 36, the vehicle displaying a new and exciting livery, using Stagecoach corporate colours but with red predominating, thereby providing a tangible link with the existing Oxford Tube image.

The new fleet was officially launched at Gloucester Green in a ceremony quite unlike anything seen previously in the bus industry. A large marquee was erected to house proceedings, and following addresses by various members of the management team the coach was unveiled, quite literally, to a gathering of journalists, bus-industry professionals and other guests, accompanied by a fanfare and smoke, and with tastefully dressed young ladies parading in front of the vehicle, to the delight of the assembled photographers. One photograph, by the then Assistant Editor of *Buses*, Philip Lamb, appeared on the front cover of the May 1999 issue, causing a minor stir amongst some of the older readers, who were not used to seeing beautiful young ladies on the front cover of the magazine!

Above: **MAN/Jonckheere No 50, with personalised registration T50 UBE, at Gloucester Green on the night of 20 June 1999, three weeks after entering service.** MALCOLM CROWE

Right: **Although the first examples had appeared in April 1999, delivery of the new fleet of MAN double-deckers took until August to complete, and some were pressed into use without branding. No 57 seen thus on 23 July, having entered service just a few days previously.** MALCOLM CROWE

Above: **MAN No 48 (T48 BBW) displaying the special destination seen on 28 December 1999.**
MALCOLM CROWE

Left: **No 48 again, this time departing Gloucester Green for Stratford-upon-Avon on 2 January 2000.**
MALCOLM CROWE

The new coaches represented an investment of over £5.5 million, and contemporary Stagecoach publicity claimed that they were the first fully accessible coaches anywhere. Although they had flat floors, seats were arranged on footstools to give passengers a better view. On eight of the coaches the first four seats on the nearside, arranged as facing pairs, were mounted on a removable plinth, allowing the carriage of a wheelchair, and these vehicles featured 'kneeling' front suspension, facilitating wheelchair access.

The new fleet gradually took to the road, replacing the conventional coaches on the Victoria service. Delivery took from April until August to complete, some of the new coaches entering service without branding.

June saw the introduction of a new timetable reflecting the introduction of the new fleet. The basic service remained as previously but at certain times of day was enhanced, the 10-minute frequency, for example, now commencing at 05.50 instead of 06.10. Another innovation was the introduction of 'The Capital Select Express', which after leaving Thornhill Park & Ride ran non-stop to Marble Arch.

It was at this time that newspapers and breakfasts were introduced. This was appropriate, because the new MAN coaches had space to lay these items out, which was not necessarily the case on a conventional coach seating around 50 passengers.

The timetable was revised again in June 1999 to include the aforementioned commuter expresses and now offered 88 services on weekdays, 82 on Saturdays and 73 on Sundays, giving a seat capacity of just under 17,000 per week in each direction. The day-return fare to Victoria was now £7.50 (£2.97 in 1987), the single £7.00 (£2.90 in 1987) and a period return

£9.50 (£4.95 in 1987). Student fares were £6.50, £6.00 and £7.00 respectively, which fares also applied to children and senior citizens. A new fare for a family of two adults and two children was priced at £22 for a day return and at £26 for a period return. A 'Tube 12' (12 single journeys with a validity of one year) cost £40, giving a return-trip cost equivalent of just £6.66. A weekly pass was now £30, a two-week ticket £53, a new three-week ticket £80, and four-week ticket £100. Longer-term prices were £310 for 13 weeks, £599 for 26 weeks (new) and £830 for an annual pass; a two-year ticket was priced at £1,500 — a real bargain for regular daily commuters. These tickets were also valid for unlimited travel on Stagecoach buses in zones 1 and 2 in Oxford.

New also at this time was a service of offering London tourists the chance to visit Stratford-upon-Avon. 'The Shakespearean' left London at 09.00, arriving in Stratford by 12.10. The return trip left Stratford at18.20 arriving back in London by 21.30. A driver change took place in Oxford. An alternative, more flexible timetable was later offered for passengers who might wish to change in Oxford. Branded the X50, the new service to Stratford-upon Avon offered seven journeys per day, excepting Sundays, leaving Gloucester Green at 50min past each odd hour, starting at 08.50

The Oxford Tube entered the new millennium with a bang, record numbers of passengers using the service as they returned from New Year celebrations in London. Almost anything with wheels was turned out to cope with the enormous numbers of passengers wishing to use the service. Low-floor MAN saloons and Leyland Olympian double-deckers were among the many vehicles from Stagecoach's Oxford bus fleet that were pressed into service to and from London,

Below: **Although it appeared to be the newest of the MAN/Jonckheere coaches, No 66 was in fact the oldest, having been used initially for development work. It is pictured at Gloucester Green shortly after entering service in July 2000.**
MALCOLM CROWE

Left: **The Monaco bodies lent themselves to rear end promotion of the service. Here No 40 (T40 UBE) speeds along the M40 bound for London.** MALCOLM CROWE

Above: **More 'Super-rear' promotional branding as applied to Nos 42 and 48, seen at Gloucester Green on 20 October 2000.** MALCOLM CROWE

Below: **Further examples of the 'super-rear' advertising applied to the MAN/ Jonckheere double-deckers, photographed in July 2001.** MALCOLM CROWE

Above: **A comparative view of Nos 37, 34 and 39, showing the different styles of branding applied to these vehicles.** MALCOLM CROWE

Left: **'Super-rear' advertisement for the Oxford May Day Ball as applied in the spring of 2000.** MALCOLM CROWE

such was the demand for seats. This set a pattern for similar special occasions in the future, but many of the record loadings experienced that night remain unsurpassed. Among other special services operated during this period were excursions from Oxford to the Millennium Dome, these services even warranting a special destination display.

Besides the principal London service the MAN double-deck coaches were put to good use on other routes; one operated an early-morning journey on bus service 31 to Wantage before returning as an express (X31), giving commuters additional capacity and greater comfort. Occasionally the double-deckers were used for private hires, weddings and such like, as well as the odd trip to South Coast resorts such as Brighton.

July 2000 saw the arrival of an additional MAN, No 66 (W66 BBW). It has been suggested that this coach was originally to have been registered T66

Top far left: **Following extensive refurbishment the MAN damaged by fire in 2002 re-entered service as No 50038, reflecting the introduction by Stagecoach of a nationwide fleet-numbering scheme. For the remainder of its time on Oxford Tube work it ran in plain red. This photograph, taken at Gloucester Green on 30 April 2004, shows clearly the modified interior décor, with blue side walls and steps and plain, light-coloured flooring.** MALCOLM CROWE

Bottom far left and this page: **No 38's revamped interior was considerably brighter than the original.** MALCOLM CROWE

UBE, this mark having been reserved, but presumably it was considered preferable to indicate that the coach was new and not one of the existing batch. Ironically it was, in fact, the original test vehicle upon which the others were modelled and was thus older than the rest!

The MANs now settled down to a period of hard work on the Victoria route, but, as explained, could also be seen in Wantage, Chipping Norton and Stratford-upon-Avon. They were popular with passengers and crews alike, offering a greater level of comfort than that experienced previously. The large unglazed area the rear provided a golden opportunity for advertising, and over the years many different and attractive advertisements were seen. Rated at 350bhp, the MAN engine was quite powerful and was also smooth and unobtrusive, particularly on the upper

deck. However, the coaches not always reliable in service, engine belts snapping on a number of occasions. The most high-profile incident befell No 38, which in late 2002 caught fire on the M40 near Lane End. The blaze caused considerable damage to the rear end of the coach, and the vehicle was out of service for some 18 months as a result. Fortunately no passengers were hurt, and the driver quickly got his charges off the coach prior to the arrival of the fire brigade.

Following its misfortune No 38 was the subject of trials to see if the MANs could be refurbished and upgraded rather than replaced by a new fleet of coaches. February 2004 saw the coach return from Plaxtons, where the work had been undertaken. Seating had been reduced to 64 — 49 (a reduction of four) on the upper deck and 15 on the lower. The moquette was renewed using a red and orange pattern, making the interior much brighter.

Meanwhile, an apparent competitor to the Oxford Tube and the COMS Oxford Espress (as it was by then known) entered the fray in August 2003. This was in fact a new concept from Stagecoach, known as Megabus, which would quickly

This spread and overleaf: **The Oxford–London Megabus service was introduced in August 2004 and by the end of the month was being operated by a dedicated fleet of Alexander-bodied tri-axle Leyland Olympians transferred from Stagecoach's Citybus operation in Hong Kong, among them No 13604.** MALCOLM CROWE

spread across the UK and to other parts of the world, and was heralded by Stagecoach as 'the world's first low-cost inter-urban bus route'. Seats would be bookable only on the megabus.com website, fares starting at just £1 each way (plus 50p booking fee). The service was to run between Oxford and London six times a day using tri-axle Leyland Olympians with 94-seat Alexander bodywork that were surplus to the requirements of

Stagecoach's Citybus operation in Hong Kong. Stagecoach went on to point out that 'this is very different from anything else being offered at the moment, and we believe that it will complement, rather than undermine, the existing coach services to London'.

Although the website was launched on Monday 4 August, the buses themselves did not start running until a week later, Monday 11 August, allowing

customers enough time to book the first departures. The service was scheduled to depart not from Gloucester Green but from Oxpens Coach Park, travelling thence via St Giles, Marston Ferry Road, to Baker Street. Sandhills and Hillingdon aside, Megabus would not serve any of the existing stops.

As the vehicles earmarked for the service were not going to be ready for the launch day, two further tri-axle Olympians, new to Stagecoach Cumberland but used more recently in Manchester and Glasgow, were drafted in for the launch. They were 14239 (WLT 727, formerly F201 FHH) and 14240 (WLT 794, ex F202 FHH).

With the service underway the designated fleet, all in Magic Bus blue with bold advertising vinyls, soon took over. They were numbered 13601/4/5 (BIW 4977, 331 HWD and SJI 4558). The trio had previously been Citybus 135/8/9 (ER 9371, ER 8635, ES 2467), and were later named *Keble, Balliol and Magdalen* — after famous Oxford colleges — respectively.

Before the end of the following year Megabus had expanded and was offering a route from Edinburgh to Glasgow, whilst a press report suggested that the trial Megabus service launched on the

popular Oxford–London route had seen 3,000 tickets sold in three weeks!

The tri-axle Olympians soon became a familiar sight on the road to London, the service being very well supported by the student population. Low-cost travel, as pioneered by budget airlines, translated very well to the UK coaching scene, and in the management corridors in Perth much discussion doubtless ensued as to how the concept should be taken forward.

4. The Skyliner era

Despite the experimental refurbishment work undertaken on coach No 38 the decision was taken not to extend the work to the other 27 MAN coaches. Instead they were to be replaced in their entirety by a fleet of brand-new vehicles. As a result trials were held in January of 2004 using Neoplan Skyliner DD53 BUZ, the first of a revised style in the UK and loaned from Buzzlines, based in Hythe, Kent. This massive coach was 13.7m long — 1.7m longer than anything used hitherto, and on a very wet night the blue tri-axle ran around the streets of Oxford to test how suitable it was for service in the city.

There followed much discussion between all interested parties, some suggesting that the type was far too big to use at Gloucester Green. However, as discussions progressed agreement to use the bus station was reached, and the focus of attention shifted to the matter of which bays should be used. It was agreed that bays 2, 3 and 4 would suitable, this being

Below: **Borrowed from Buzz Lines to assess the type's suitability for Oxford Tube service, 13.7m Neoplan Skyliner DD53 BUZ rounds the Carfax on the evening of 15 January 2004.**
MALCOLM CROWE

achieved by relocating the Bicester services and amalgamating the three bays into two, to allow ample room for the loading of wheelchairs through the rear door.

Ultimately an order was placed with Neoplan for a batch of 25 Skyliners with seating for 81 passengers (61 on the upper deck and 20 on the lower), the total being reduced to 79 when a wheelchair was carried. A ramp was provided to facilitate entry of a wheelchair through the rear door, and the rearmost nearside seat folded and provided space for the wheelchair. This arrangement was ideal and at last made long-distance coach travel truly accessible to the wheelchair user. In addition to being fully wheelchair-accessible and equipped with washroom facilities and air-conditioning, the new coaches featured reclining seats (with seatbelts) allowing generous legroom and with power points for laptops and mobile phones; they were also equipped with CCTV technology for additional passenger security.

The Skyliners were built at the Neoplan factory in Stuttgart, Germany, and the author was fortunate enough to be in the area when the third coach (fleet number 50103) was being prepared for delivery. Heralding a new era for the Oxford Tube, replacement of the fleet allowed for more than 6,000 passengers a day to travel

Above: **Striking vehicles by any standards, the Neoplan Skyliners heralded a new era for the Oxford Tube. No 50103 was photographed on 11 May 2004 prior to delivery from Stuttgart.** MALCOLM CROWE

Above: **By the time this picture was taken on 19 June 2004 at the Network Oxford industrial estate, five Neoplans were available for training. The prominent lettering was designed to ensure that everyone knew about the new fleet...**
MALCOLM CROWE

Right: **Inside, the rearmost pair of seats on the nearside tipped up, making it very easy to accommodate a wheelchair. Any accompanying passenger could be seated alongside.** MALCOLM CROWE

on the service to London and was achieved at a cost of £8 million — at that time the UK's largest investment in new vehicles for a single route.

Delivery of the coaches, Nos 50101-25 (KP04 GJE-G/J/K/U/V/X-Z, GKA-G/J-N, T40/4, 50/5, 60 UBE) was spread over several months, being completed in September 2004. Driver training had begun in June in readiness for a formal launch in August, a mixed fleet continuing in operation in the interim.

With the introduction of the Skyliners the MANs found new lives with Stagecoach on Megabus services in Scotland, those originally with T-UBE registrations (Nos 40/4, 50/5, 60) being re-registered T614-8 DWL respectively before departure.

Somewhat overshadowed by the arrival of the Skyliners, by June 2004 another tri-axle Olympian, the first to have a toilet fitted, had been transferred to Oxford for Megabus duties. Numbered 13618 (H522 FRP), it had previously been Citybus 131 (ER 9169) and was named *Trinity*.

A new timetable introduced on 12 December 2004 listed 79 return journeys on weekdays, 78 on Saturdays and 74 on

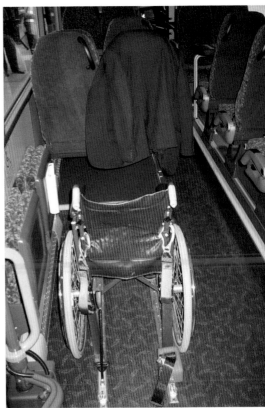

Sundays. These included three express commuter journeys from Oxford to London every weekday morning at 06.00, 06.24 and 07.00 and one returning from London at 09.25. The author recalls that this last

Above: **No 50103 on crew-training duty in Central London on 11 June 2004.** MALCOLM CROWE

Left: **The Neoplans were soon to be seen in London on crew training, as demonstrated by this example passing Marble Arch on 11 June 2004.** MALCOLM CROWE

operated via Baker Street and The Westway to avoid passing intending passengers at Notting Hill Gate or Shepherds Bush; furthermore it did not call at Hillingdon and Lewknor. Arrival in Oxford was timed for 11.00. This working would survive only until the introduction of the next new timetable, in December 2005.

A welcome addition was the Taxi-bus service connecting with the Oxford Tube at Lewknor and run by Walters Limousines. This was sponsored by Oxford and Buckinghamshire county councils and offered connections from Chalgrove, Cuxham, Watlington, Chinnor, Kingston Blount and Aston Rowant for passengers travelling to Oxford or London. Later the service also included Stokenchurch, but sadly it never really got off the ground. Indeed a Bucks County council official

admitted that for Stokenchurch each passenger carried represented a cost of £40.

At the start of 2005 the number of seats offered per week was nearly 20,000 in one direction — a substantial increase over the 1999 figure. The day-return fare was now £11.00 (£7.50 in 1999), the single £9.00 (compared with £7.00) and a period return £13.00 (up from £11.00). Student fares were £8.00, £7.00 and £10.00 respectively — these fares also applied to children and senior citizens. Introduced at this time was a revised fare for a family of two adults and three children of £24 for a day return and £28 for a period return. These fares were a real bargain, having increased only marginally since 1999. A 'Tube 12' (12 single journeys with a validity of one year) cost £47, giving a return-trip price equivalent of just £7.83.

Above: **Tri-axle Leyland Olympian/Alexander No 13601 calls at Hillingdon on the afternoon of 14 May 2004.** MALCOLM CROWE

Top far left: **Displaced from Oxford Tube work by the Neoplan Skyliners, the MANs saw further service with Stagecoach in Scotland. On 6 March 2007 No 50059, by now in Motorvator livery, was photographed on the 900 Glasgow–Edinburgh service.** CHRIS MAXFIELD

Bottom far left: **No 50052 in City Link livery on the Glasgow–Edinburgh service.** CHRIS MAXFIELD

Left: **Timetable for the Lewknor Taxibus service, introduced early in 2005.** MALCOLM CROWE

Above: **The new bus shelters installed at Lewknor, complete with phones enabling passengers to call the Taxibuses.** MALCOLM CROWE

Above right: **Signs on the B4009 direct drivers to the bus interchange at Lewknor.** MALCOLM CROWE

A weekly pass was now £37, a two-week ticket £65, a three-week ticket £97 and a four-week ticket £120. Longer times were 13 weeks for £345, 26 weeks for £670 and finally an annual pass was now £910. A two-year ticket was priced at £1,650, still a real bargain for those regular daily commuters. As before, these tickets gave unlimited travel on Stagecoach Oxford in its Zones 1 and 2.

During May 2005 four of the Jonckheere-bodied MANs, now Stagecoach 50040/6/7/58 (T614 DWL, T46/7, 58 BBW) returned for a short period to cover for post-delivery modifications to all 25 members of the Neoplan fleet. The work took about six weeks and was carried out at three locations on four coaches at a time. The MANs were in excellent condition, and as the Oxford Tube also carries Megabus passengers they did not look too out of place on the service in their new livery. Among other duties the MANs were used on the early-morning 31/X31 return journey that was operated by an Oxford Tube coach.

On Saturday 2 July 2005 the Oxford Tube operated extra vehicles to provide additional capacity for travellers heading to and from the Live 8 concert in Hyde Park. Park Lane was closed southbound between 08.30 and 13.00 for a parade at 12.00.

Coaches were diverted via Kensington Church Street, passengers for Marble Arch being advised to alight at either Notting Hill Gate or Victoria station. The streets surrounding Hyde Park were closed from 19.00 until the crowds from the concert dispersed. During that time coaches were diverted via the Embankment and Shepherd's Bush, serving the Kensington Hilton stop via Royal Crescent. Passengers travelling from London during these diversions were advised to board at Grosvenor Gardens, as the Tube was unable to stop at Notting Hill Gate or Marble Arch. On that day 33 coaches and buses were used on the London Oxford Tube service, the total comprising 24 of the 25 Skyliners (the missing example being 50123, away at Rotherham for modification work), all four of the MAN/Jonckheere Monaco coaches then on loan and five Alexander-bodied Volvo Olympians — 16521-4/6 (R421-4/6 XFC) — borrowed from Stagecoach's Oxford bus fleet. The services of both Oxford–London operators were fully subscribed from around 08.30 until 12.30, and passengers joining after the St Clements stop had to wait quite some time for space on coaches. By contrast, at around 21.00 some 15 Oxford Tube coaches and Stagecoach buses were awaiting passengers returning from London.

On Sunday 18 September 2005 Skyliner No 50124 (T55 UBE) attended the Showbus rally, held annually at the Imperial War

Above: **The Skyliners' interior was typically Stagecoach with monogrammed blue moquette and red flooring.** MALCOLM CROWE

Left: **No 50121 at Gloucester Green on 3 September 2004, before overall branding was applied. The destination display, originally scrolling, was later made static following complaints from motorists who found it distracting.** MALCOLM CROWE

Left: **Temporarily back in Oxford Tube service, MAN No 50046 leaves Central London on the morning of 18 May 2005.** MALCOLM CROWE

Bottom left and below: **The spring of 2005 saw the return on loan of four of the MAN/Jonckheere Monacos, two of which are seen parked at the Excel Logistics depot in Oxford on 17 May.** MALCOLM CROWE/MARTIN BANHAM

Bottom: **No 50047 in Wantage on the 07.20 to Oxford on 6 June 2005.** GAVIN FRANCIS

Top far left: **At vary busy times, virtually any suitable vehicle available is pressed into service. Here Stagecoach in Oxfordshire 18198 (KN54 ZXO), an Alexander-bodied Dennis Trident from the Brooks University dedicated fleet rests in Buckingham Palace Road.** CHRIS MAXFIELD

Bottom far left: **The Live 8 pop concert staged in Hyde Park on 2 June 2005 saw all available vehicles draughted into Oxford Tube service, including a number from Stagecoach's Oxford bus fleet. Volvo Olympian/ Alexander No 16521 is seen at the Buckingham Palace Road terminus, with another of the type behind.** BEN MORROLL

Left: **Having already made a round-trip earlier in the day, MAN No 50040 leaves Oxford on the afternoon of 2 June, running empty to London to collect returning crowds.** MALCOLM CROWE

Museum site at Duxford, where more than 500 vehicles, historic and contemporary, were on display. It won two awards — Best Modern Vehicle and Best New Millennium Coach. On the previous day the author, along with Harvey Cullimore, a then drivers' mentor and members of the engineering staff at the Horspath depot, had spent nearly 12 hours preparing the coach, this despite the fact that the engineering team had already put in a considerable number of hours on the preceding Thursday and Friday; indeed, it is only when one gets down to cleaning a vehicle used in everyday service that one realises how much effort is required on a regular basis to keep it in tip-top condition. It was also interesting to note that, in the judging, account is taken of the vehicle's regular work and hence the intensity of use. As if to prove a point, shortly after returning to Oxford on the Sunday evening No 50124 was off to London on the night service.

Following its success at Showbus No 50124 went along to represent modern vehicles at the 2005 Amersham running day. It proved very popular and during the course of the day was used in service to Slough, Windsor and Gerrards Cross, mainly working service 353, with appropriate destination displays.

On Wednesday 9 November the Hilton Hotel in Park Lane hosted the annual UK Bus Awards, this being the 10th-anniversary event. Many operators entered the event, and Stagecoach was successful in three categories. Stagecoach West Scotland was declared overall winner and won the Larger Fleets award, but nearer to home, the Oxford Tube won the Claudia Flanders Memorial Award for Accessibility, the judges commenting: 'Long distance coach travel can be difficult for disabled people and has so often been impossible for those who need to use wheelchairs. In addition to the fully accessible fleet for the Oxford Tube service the staff training measures, publicity and new website combine to provide a truly accessible service around the clock'.

The Megabus service from Oxford to London also continued to enjoy unprecedented success. By now some journeys were being operated by Stagecoach East London's Leyton garage, resulting in the appearance of bus-seated Dennis Tridents; intending

Above: **Skyliner No 50124 arrives at Showbus 2005, with the author at the wheel.** GAVIN FRANCIS

Right: **The spoils of victory. Harvey Cullimore (right) and the author pose in front of No 50124.** GAVIN FRANCIS

Above: **Neoplan Skyliner 50124 (T55 UBE) is seen outside the Kings Arms in Stokenchurch on its way to the Amersham Running Day on 2 October 2005.**
MALCOLM CROWE

Far left and left:
Wheelchair access on the Neoplan Skyliner.
MALCOLM CROWE

passengers booking on megabus.com were able to choose from selected journeys operated by The Oxford Tube but in London could board only at Gloucester Green in Oxford or Buckingham Palace Road, the terminus of the Oxford Tube since Saturday 13 September 2003. Additionally the Megabus departure-point in Oxford had been moved from Oxpens to Gloucester Green. This brought many new passengers to the Oxford Tube, filling potentially empty seats, notably on the Capital Select journeys departing at 06.00 and 06.30. This change meant that Megabus passengers could enjoy an enhanced service, always travelling on a coach.

Right and below right:
Pressed into Megabus service, Volvo Olympian No 16523 seen loading at Gloucester Green on 20 November 2004 and later the same day inside Stagecoach East London's Leyton garage while on layover in the capital.
MALCOLM CROWE

On Saturdays, however, no Megabus seats were available on Oxford Tube coaches leaving Gloucester Green between 08.26 and 11.36 hours. Instead there were two duplicate Megabus journeys departing at 09.30 and 11.00 for the use of Megabus passengers. Similarly, on return journeys from London no Megabus seats were available on Oxford Tube coaches leaving Buckingham Palace Road between 17.48 and 20.05 hours, Megabus providing duplicates 18.00 and 19.30. The Saturday Megabus 'dupes' were operated by Volvo Olympians from the Stagecoach's Oxford bus fleet. On arrival at Victoria they ran 'dead' to Leyton, returning to Victoria for their timed departures back to Oxford. These extras ran until a week before Christmas 2004 but did not reappear thereafter.

Although the Megabus service has today been fully integrated into the Oxford Tube, and the Megabus-liveried vehicles have gone, a proportion of passengers still use the Oxford Tube service with tickets booked on megabus.com. A few restrictions apply, one being that tickets cannot be booked on the peak commuter services, another that passengers holding Megabus tickets cannot bring bicycles. Megabus passengers may board at any stop *en route* but are not guaranteed a place unless they board at either terminus.

Monday 16 January 2006 saw another milestone in the history of the Oxford Tube, when the breakfast service was upgraded. That morning travellers on the journey to London tucked into an improved complementary breakfast that consisted of hot bacon baguettes, cheese-and-tomato baguettes, pain au chocolat and croissants, as well as fruit juices. Available for every passenger to enjoy after boarding his or her coach,

the breakfasts were prepared by Harvey's of Oxford, which ensured that between 05.40 and 07.00 each morning Oxford Tube coaches were stocked with hot food fresh from its ovens. Flavio Zappi of Harvey's said: 'It's great to be in partnership with Oxford Tube, and we are very proud that all these passengers are trying our great food'. Phil Rumsby, a passenger who had been travelling on the Oxford Tube since it started, said:

'The new breakfasts are even better than the previous ones. The service has always been good, but the new breakfast gives that additional edge which makes the journey even more pleasant'.

The Lewknor Taxibus service had been due to finish at the end of January but was granted a reprieve. This was indeed good news, but in a press release Oxford County Council warned that people must make good use of the service.

Come the summer of 2006 a prolonged heatwave caused a few problems with the Skyliners, which therefore required urgent modification. To help provide continuity two Leyland Olympians normally used in connection with South West Trains were borrowed at short notice from Stagecoach South, arriving on Friday 21 July and were used to bolster capacity on the Oxford Tube while the Skyliners were being modified. The work was completed within three weeks, and two Oxford drivers, one being the author, returned the Olympians to their home depot at Winchester on Friday 11 August.

From August 2006 a timetable alteration made provision for the 06.00 express commuter service to call at Lewknor, the objective being to provide

an additional journey from Lewknor to London. From April 2007, however, this journey reverted to running non-stop, as Lewknor was now served by journeys timed at 05.25 and 05.40, as well as the existing 05.10 and 05.50 departures.

Another coup for Stagecoach was the introduction of Wi-Fi access on Oxford Tube coaches from 1 October 2006 — the first time such a service had been offered in the UK. The 25 vehicles in the fleet were equipped with technology supplied by Telabria Networks, and the system was ready for operation as a pilot scheme from 1 October. The trial of the Wi-Fi technology also included the first major deployment of Telabria's mTracker vehicle-tracking system. This gave Stagecoach a real-time at-a-glance view of its fleet and precise locations of individual vehicles on the road via the web. Brian Souter, Chief Executive of Stagecoach Holdings, said at the time: 'We have made a huge investment in the

Oxford Tube over the past two years, and this new Wi-Fi pilot puts Stagecoach at the forefront of offering next-generation on-board services for coach customers. Many of our passengers on the Oxford Tube are commuters and students, so having free access to E-mail and the Internet will be a significant benefit. The technology will also help us track the progress of vehicles on the network and advise customers of any issues that are likely to affect our services.'

Jim Baker, Founder and Chief Executive Officer of Telabria Networks, added: 'Access to a broadband connection is becoming increasingly important for travellers. Telabria's MobilAPi mobile broadband router delivers Wi-Fi service to passengers, connecting to the Internet via the latest generation of cellular data networks at broadband speeds. We are delighted that Stagecoach has chosen our market-leading technology to deploy across the Oxford Tube fleet, raising the bar for cutting-edge passenger services.'

Above: **Skyliner No 50125 with Olympians 13646 and 13652 at Victoria on 26 July 2006.** CHRIS MAXFIELD

Top far left: **Phil Rumsby, a regular commuter, is served one of the new fabulous breakfasts by Flavio Zappi, Manager of Harvey's.** STAGECOACH

Far left: **Tri-axle Leyland Olympians Nos 13652 and 13646 parked at Horspath Road on 21 July 2006.** MALCOLM CROWE

The results of the trial having been assessed, the system was soon made available on a permanent basis, and to promote the benefits of the new facility to passengers, both existing and prospective, revised branding was applied to Skyliner No 50108. A secure E-commerce website, www.oxfordtube.com, was also introduced at this time, allowing customers to book single, return and period tickets online as well as accessing timetable and service information.

The week ending 14 October saw at least two Skyliners (Nos 50108 and 50117) sporting revised branding publicising the Wi-Fi facility on the Oxford Tube. Additionally there were a number of rear-end schemes, all of which were *in situ* by early 2007, whilst lettering applied to the upper-deck side windows pronounced very clearly the advantages of using the Oxford Tube. Another innovation at this

time was the introduction of a recorded boarding and arrival announcement giving safety details and, in particular, asking passengers to ensure that their seatbelts were fastened.

Above: **Wi-Fi connections help commuters to work on their journey to London.** MALCOLM CROWE

Far left: **'Wi-Fi is here' — the original style of branding as applied to No 50108.** MALCOLM CROWE

Bottom far left: **By the spring of 2007 five styles of rear-end branding were in evidence. This photograph was taken on 24 May.** MALCOLM CROWE

Left: **Passengers boarding the 06.24 express (non-stop to Marble Arch) at Thornhill, 24 May 2007. They will arrive in London by 08.30 having read the morning paper, enjoyed a breakfast and had time to catch up on their E-mails.** MALCOLM CROWE

Right: **Seen approaching Stokenchurch well loaded, No 50133 was clearly being put to good use on (Bank Holiday) Monday 25 August 2008.** MALCOLM CROWE

Far right: **No 50133 earlier on the morning of 25 August, pictured alongside native Skyliner No 50113 (right).** GAVIN FRANCIS

Below: **Aboard the 06.24 express from Oxford to London in May 2007. Note the lettering on the upper-deck side windows, informing prospective passengers of the advantages of using the Oxford Tube.** MALCOLM CROWE

Below right: **More happy commuters in May 2007. The breakfast trays can be seen on the left of the picture.** MALCOLM CROWE

Following delivery of the Oxford batch, Stagecoach had in 2005 received a further 25 Neoplan Skyliners, these being allocated throughout the country for use Megabus services, but the arrival (from 2007) of batches of 15m tri-axle Volvo B12B/ Plaxton Panther coaches saw most reallocated to Stagecoach Express services in Scotland. However, in August 2008 an increased vehicle requirement on the Oxford Tube saw one arrive on extended loan, the vehicle in question being

No 50133 (CN05 APV), which had been new to the group's Red & White subsidiary in South Wales. By now in standard Stagecoach colours (rather than Megabus blue), it was given appropriate decals for its year-long stay in Oxford. In common with the other Megabus Skyliners it had 89 seats (eight more than an Oxford Tube example) and thus proved especially useful in coping with increased passenger numbers at busy times, notably weekends; on the debit side it lacked a centre door and so could not carry wheelchairs, and a number of drivers did not like it, being convinced that the cab was smaller than that of their regular steeds! It did, however, serve its purpose, resulting in a fleet of 26 coaches being available for service.

Below: **A Megabus Skyliner in London on an Edinburgh working.** MALCOLM CROWE

Below: **A Megabus Skyliner in London on an Edinburgh working.** MALCOLM CROWE

5. Van Hool — the choice for the latest Tube fleet

When the Skyliners were introduced in the summer of 2004 they represented a significant step forward for the Oxford Tube service, bringing more seats and wheelchair accessibility for every coach. When delivered they had boasted (amongst many other modern enhancements requested by passengers) power points for each pair of seats, and during their time in service they were modified to offer Wi-Fi to all customers. However, by 2009 their time on the route was drawing to a close, and rumours were rife regarding their replacements, which were expected to enter service between June and September. Many questions were asked but lips were sealed, and little information was forthcoming from those understood to be in the know.

Most of the Skyliners had covered more than a million kilometres (650,000 miles) during their five-year stint with the Oxford Tube, having seen very heavy utilisation, and by May 2009 preparations were in hand in anticipation of their

Below: **Skyliner No 50125 re-registered in readiness for disposal.** GAVIN FRANCIS

Left and below left: **First of the Oxford Tube Van Hool Astromegas to arrive in the UK was No 50202, which during the week of 8 June 2009 was observed on test in and around Oxford on Belgian trade plates! It subsequently returned to Van Hool in Belgium for various modifications to be incorporated prior to delivery of the batch.** MALCOLM CROWE

replacements. The first outward sign of this was the removal of the personalised numberplates carried hitherto by Nos 50121-5; these were removed during the week ending Friday 23 May and replaced with registrations OX04 BZT/U/S/P/R respectively.

It was confirmed by Stagecoach on Monday 8 June that the new fleet would consist of 26 Van Hool TD927 Astromega integral double-deckers, left-hand drive examples of which had already been built for service in the USA, where Megabus operated a large fleet of coaches on inter-state services. The first for Oxford Tube, No 50202, had in fact already arrived in the UK late the previous day direct from the factory in Belgium, running on Belgian trade plates. It had been sent to test a number of matters concerning in-service requirements and was used on test runs for the whole of the following week before returning to Belgium for final preparations to be completed.

Stagecoach extolled the virtues of the new coaches in its press release, which

announced that they would be fitted with DAF EEV (Enhanced Environmental Vehicles) engines giving even lower emissions than those required by the Euro 5 standard coming into force later in the year. It went on to state: 'A Selective Catalytic Reduction (SCR) system uses a constant feed of urea solution to destroy the harmful NOx, delivering a more efficient operation of the engine, reduced diesel consumption and lower running costs. Combined with a passive soot filter, it means the vehicles are even cleaner than those fitted with compressed-natural-gas engines'. You can't argue with that ...

The 87-seat fully accessible vehicles, this time with two staircases, were, like their predecessors, equipped with washroom facilities, air-conditioning, reclining seats with generous legroom, seatbelts, power points for laptops and mobile phones, GPS tracking and CCTV for personal security. Carried over from their predecessors was the provision of an in-coach safety recording played following departure and an arrival announcement near the end of each journey, this requiring the driver merely to announce the stops and add appropriate information in case of a delay or diversion.

Deliveries of the new fleet, worth £9 million (almost £350,000 per vehicle) began at the beginning of July. The first five coaches, Nos 50201-5, were given the personalised registrations (T40/4, 50/5, 60 UBE), the next 10, Nos 50206-15, receiving locally issued registrations (OU09 FMY/Z/A/NC-H/J). The next four vehicles on the production line (from a total Stagecoach order for 30 coaches

Left: **Astromega No 50203 passes beneath Botley Road bridge on the morning of 13 July 2009, the first day of crew training.** GAVIN FRANCIS

Below: **Another view of No 50203, this time reversing off Bay 3 at Gloucester Green.** GAVIN FRANCIS

— 26 for the Oxford Tube, plus a further four vehicles for the Megabus operation) were originally intended as part of the Oxford Tube allocation but were diverted to Megabus for use on Anglo-Scottish services and allocated to Aberdeen. As a result all of the remaining 11 coaches now went to the Oxford Tube as its Nos 50216-26, and being delivered after 1 September received '59' plates (OU59 AVC-E, AUR, AUO/T/V-Y, AVB). Deliveries were completed by the end of the month, Nos 50216-9 being the last four coaches off the line, taking the fleet numbers allocated originally to the four vehicles diverted to Megabus.

Upon delivery Nos 50202-5 were allocated initially to driver training, which encompassed not only the drivers on the London service but also engineering and depot staff, who would need to shunt the coaches at Horspath — there was a great deal to be achieved before the Astromegas could enter service.

Drivers' first impressions were that they were very nice coaches to drive, the transmission, in particular, being a great improvement over that fitted to the Skyliners, especially in the London traffic. Despite a slight increase in length (of 0.5m) they handled very well indeed. Reversing at Gloucester Green was found to be much easier on account of a

Top: **A group of disadvantaged young people and children, some with disabilities, were among the first to ride on the new £9 million fleet of luxury coaches for Stagecoach's Oxford Tube on Saturday 1 August 2009.** STAGECOACH

Above: **The coaches and drivers are ready to take lucky travellers for their day in London.** STAGECOACH

Right: **Coaches used were Nos 50207, 50208 and 50212 on the free service and No 50205 for the children's trip.** STAGECOACH

Above: **No 50205 arrives at Thornhill from London, with Gavin Francis at the wheel.** PETER EDGAR

Left: **The old and the new in Buckingham Palace Road on 3 August.** GAVIN FRANCIS

steering rear axle which brings the back around more easily when in reverse; the Skyliner's trailing axle steered only when driven forward. The steering wheel itself is smaller, which helps when making awkward turns, that on the Skyliner having been reminiscent of a large dinner plate!

The company was anxious to take full advantage of the new fleet of Astromegas and arranged two special events to be held on 1 August, before the coaches' official entry into service. Firstly 261 day-return tickets from Oxford to London were given away; these were available on a 'first come, first served' basis, and lucky ticket-holders were able to claim

up to four seats each. Then, at 09.00, special coaches departed the coach park next to Oxford Ice Rink for a high-speed run to London, travelling non-stop as far as Hillingdon, following which it was possible to disembark at Shepherd's Bush, Notting Hill, Marble Arch and, of course, Victoria; passengers were then free to return on any journey that day.

On the same day the Oxford Tube teamed up with Oxfordshire County Council and Merlin Entertainments, a company behind some of London's biggest attractions, to give 64 children a special day out in the capital. Travelling on one of the Astromegas, the group was taken first

Below: Shortly after the Astromegas entered service road works in London's West End resulted in the extraordinary sight of coaches being diverted through Hyde Park. No 50209 is seen emerging at Cumberland Gate on 5 August 2009.
GAVIN FRANCIS

to the Science Museum before obtaining free entry to the London Eye and the SeaLife London Aquarium courtesy of children's charity Merlin's Magic Wand. Said Martin Sutton, Managing Director of Stagecoach Oxfordshire: 'We are delighted to be able to offer this thank-you to the local community, which has supported Oxford Tube's vital link to London over many years. These deserving local youngsters will be amongst the first to experience luxury travel on our new state-of-the-art coaches.'

With 15 of the new coaches delivered, the first day in revenue-earning service was scheduled for the following Monday, 3 August. They were very well received, regular passengers commenting on their space and quietness. Their size meant that they could certainly not be missed!

No sooner had the new coaches entered service than an unusual diversion was put in place in London whilst Bayswater Road was resurfaced. North

Ride was opened to traffic during the road closure. Normally coaches are banned from Hyde Park and all its roads, so for the first time Oxford Tube coaches were seen in Hyde Park. By Thursday 6 August, the diversion had been removed and the coaches reverted to their normal route.

Having had great success with a Skyliner at Showbus in 2005, the company agreed that one of the Astromegas, No 50223 (OU59 AUW), could attend the 2009 event, to be held on Sunday 27 September. The weather was glorious, and everyone enjoyed the day with again around 500 buses and coaches to look at. The coach was invited to be the 2009 representative in the *Buses 60* parade from Cambridge to Duxford, which preceded the main event, and later won an award for being the best Stagecoach vehicle.

The Skyliners were gradually prepared for return to Dawson Rentals, from which they had been leased, and departed the

Above: **No 50204 arriving at Duxford on Sunday 27 September 2009. It was later adjudged the best Stagecoach vehicle at the show.** GARY SEAMARKS

Above: **Ex-Tube Skyliners at Plaxtons, Anston, on 21 October 2009. Many have already been repainted.**
CLIVE MIDDLETON

Right: **No 50121 at Anston on 21 October 2009 — repainted but still displaying the Oxford Tube logo on the front.**
CLIVE MIDDLETON

Left: **The winter of 2009/10 saw adverse weather conditions affect the Oxford Tube. On 18 December the state of the M40 motorway was such that services were diverted via the parallel A40 trunk road, hence this view of Astromega No 50202 passing through High Wycombe.** GAVIN FRANCIS

Left: **Horspath depot early on 10 January 2010, and the fleet is ready for a snowy day.** GAVIN FRANCIS

Below: **The Oxford Tube managed to maintain its service to and from London — sometimes at an increased headway, but passengers always got through (and back). Here three Astromegas await their next duty in Park End Street. Coaches were run empty to London to ensure capacity on return journeys during the evening peak.** JOHN HAMMOND

fleet over a period of six weeks or so, being despatched to Plaxtons at Anston, where they were repainted all-white and generally tided up for their next owners.

The new fleet settled down to hard work, and 2009 drew to a close. By now the number of passengers using the service overnight, especially at weekends, had increased considerably, and it was not unusual for an Oxford-bound coach to depart the capital at 04.05 filled with returning revellers.

January 2010 saw atrocious weather to the South of England, Oxfordshire being no exception. This followed a bad winter in 2008/9, and the roads were once again in poor condition and in many cases treacherous.

Hazardous conditions notwithstanding, the Oxford Tube has always enjoyed an excellent safety record, but a most unfortunate incident occurred on the night of Monday 30 August 2010 when a passenger caused the driver to swerve, resulting in the vehicle's overturning near Junction 2 on the M40. Fortunately no one was seriously injured, and the coach later returned to service following repairs. The incident could have been much worse, but for the strength and construction of the new coaches.

The end of 2010 brought fresh travel problems caused by heavy snowfalls, and an emergency timetable was introduced, coaches operating to a 30min frequency, departing at 05 and 35min past the hour from Oxford and from London. The year drew to a close with a special service running via Heathrow Airport on a two-hourly basis with a minimum one-way fare of £25. The coaches were generally full, extras being run as required.

After the dramas of the previous year, 2011 proved remarkably uneventful, although a high-point in November saw Oxford Tube named Express Coach Operator of the Year at the UK Bus Awards, the judges citing the standard of operations and continued success in attracting new passengers.

Maintaining the spirit of ongoing innovation, at the beginning of 2012 the Oxford Tube returned to Bicester, two express journeys being run from Oxford each morning for the benefit of commuters

Overall, the service now offers 75 journeys on weekdays, 80 on Saturdays and 72 on Sundays. These are single Oxford–London journeys, so the number of return seats equates to just under 92,000 per week, compared with just over 17,000 per week in 1987. This translates to a staggering total of just under 5 million seats per year — well over five times the number seats offered 25 years ago!

On the vehicle front, the fleet has been replaced three times since Stagecoach took over in 1997, and on each occasion double-deck coaches have been specified. On each occasion also the opportunity has been taken to make significant improvements, and the service now

boasts fully air-conditioned vehicles equipped with 87 reclining seats and washroom facilities and offering easy access for wheelchair users.

One can only speculate as to what the future will bring, but given the ever-increasing cost of private motoring and rail travel it seems reasonable to assume that the Oxford Tube can look forward to a period of continuing success — passengers are guaranteed a seat on a service which runs every day of the year, and there's never a last coach. Here's to the next 25 years!

Appendix 1:
Oxford Tube uniforms

When the service started back in March 1987 drivers were issued with a red blazer, black-and-red striped tie, white shirt with epaulettes and black trousers. This uniform remained in use until the introduction of the Neoplan Skyliners in August 2004, when it was replaced by a grey suit, maroon tie complete with 'Oxford Tube' logotype, grey shirt and maroon pullover. The introduction of the Astromega fleet in 2009 brought a further change, the current uniform comprising a blue blazer, dark-blue trousers, blue tie with gold 'Oxford Tube' logo, white shirt and navy-blue 'naval style' sweater with blue epaulettes denoting the rank of the wearer — one bar for a driver, two for either a mentor or a deputy controller and three for a controller. Yellow high-visibility jackets have been in use from the start.

The three versions of the Oxford Tube uniform as modelled by the author. COURTESY MALCOLM CROWE

Appendix 2:
Fleet list

No	Registration	Chassis	Body	Seats	New	In	Out	Notes
1	AOD 648Y	Leyland Tiger TRCTL11/3R	Plaxton Paramount 3200	C46Ft	Apr 83	Mar 87	Jan 94	ex Devon General (2200)
2	AOD 649Y	Leyland Tiger TRCTL11/3R	Plaxton Paramount 3200	C46Ft	Apr 83	Mar 87	Jan 94	ex Devon General (2201)
3	B400 UOD	Leyland Tiger TRCTL11/3RH	Duple Laser 2	C44Ft	Jan 85	Mar 87	Jan 92	ex Devon General (2210)
4	B401 UOD	Leyland Tiger TRCTL11/3RH	Duple Laser 2	C44Ft	Jan 85	Mar 87	Aug 93	ex Devon General (2211)
5	B402 UOD	Leyland Tiger TRCTL11/3RH	Duple Laser 2	C44Ft	Jan 85	Mar 87	Jan 92	ex Devon General (2212)
6	B403 UOD	Leyland Tiger TRCTL11/3RH	Duple Laser 2	C44Ft	Jan 85	Mar 87	Dec 91	ex Devon General (2213)
7	B405 UOD	Leyland Tiger TRCTL11/3RH	Duple Laser 2	C44Ft	Jan 85	Mar 87	Jan 94	ex Devon General (2215)
8	B406 UOD	Leyland Tiger TRCTL11/3RH	Duple Laser 2	C44Ft	Jan 85	Mar 87	Apr 96	ex Devon General (2216)
9	D142 PTT	Leyland Tiger TRCTL11/3RZ	Plaxton Paramount III 3500	C51Ft	Jul 87	Jul 87	Apr 95	
10	PYV 277	Leyland Tiger TRCTL11/3RZ	Plaxton Paramount II 3500	C53F	Jul 86	Nov 87	Oct 94	ex South Midland (128), originally registered C128 KJO;
11	LSV 670	Leyland Tiger TRCTL11/3RZ	Plaxton Paramount II 3500	C53F	Jul 86	Nov 87	Nov 94	ex South Midland (129), originally registered C129 KJO;
12	EBW 101Y	Leyland Tiger TRCTL11/3R	Duple Dominant IV Express	C50F	Mar 83	Mar 88	Dec 91	ex South Midland (125); new to City of Oxford (101)
13	EBW 102Y	Leyland Tiger TRCTL11/3R	Duple Dominant IV Express	C50F	Mar 83	Mar 88	Dec 91	ex South Midland (126); new to City of Oxford (102)
920	VUD 28X	Leyland Leopard PSU3G/4R	ECW	C49F	Apr 82	Mar 88	Mar 90	ex South Midland (105) new to City of Oxford (28)
921	VUD 29X	Leyland Leopard PSU3G/4R	ECW	C49F	Apr 82	Mar 88	Mar 89	ex South Midland (106) new to City of Oxford (29)
922	VUD 30X	Leyland Leopard PSU3G/4R	ECW	C49F	Apr 82	Mar 88	Oct 89	ex South Midland (107) new to City of Oxford (30)
923	VUD 32X	Leyland Leopard PSU3G/4R	ECW	C49F	Apr 82	Mar 88	Nov 89	ex South Midland (108) new to City of Oxford (32)
14	B404 UOD	Leyland Tiger TRCTL11/3RH	Duple Laser 2	C44Ft	Jan 85	Nov 87	Mar 94	ex Devon General (2214)
15	C922 HYA	Leyland Tiger TRCTL11/3RH	Plaxton Paramount II 3500	C49Ft	May 86	Aug 89	Nov 94	ex Southern National (SN2)
16	B896 YYD	Leyland Tiger TRCTL11/3RH	Plaxton Paramount II 3200	C48Ft	Feb 85	Oct 90	Apr 95	ex Southern National (SN6)
17	B894 YYD	Leyland Tiger TRCTL11/3RH	Plaxton Paramount II 3200	C48Ft	Feb 85	Oct 90	Nov 94	ex Southern National (SN4)
18 *	H69 CFJ	Volvo B10M-60	Plaxton Paramount III 3200	C53Ft	Oct 90	Oct 90	Apr 94	
19	H913 FTT	Volvo B10M-60	Ikarus Blue Danube	C49Ft	May 91	May 91	Oct 96	
20	H914 FTT	Volvo B10M-60	Ikarus Blue Danube	C49Ft	May 91	May 91	Mar 97	
21	H915 FTT	Volvo B10M-60	Ikarus Blue Danube	C49Ft	May 91	May 91	Apr 93	
22	H916 FTT	Volvo B10M-60	Ikarus Blue Danube	C49Ft	May 91	May 91	Jun 97	
23	H917 FTT	Volvo B10M-60	Ikarus Blue Danube	C49Ft	May 91	May 91	Sep 96	
24	J499 MOD	Volvo B10M-60	Ikarus Blue Danube	C49Ft	Sep 91	Sep 91	Jul 97	

No	Registration	Chassis	Body	Seats	New	In	Out	Notes
25	H914 PTG	Volvo B10M-60	Ikarus Blue Danube	C49Ft	Apr 91	Feb 92	Apr 95	ex Hills, Tredegar
26	H915 PTG	Volvo B10M-60	Ikarus Blue Danube	C49Ft	Apr-91	Apr 92	Apr 95	ex Hills, Tredegar
27	H916 PTG	Volvo B10M-60	Ikarus Blue Danube	C49Ft	Apr-91	Feb 92	Apr 95	ex Hills, Tredegar
28	H917 PTG	Volvo B10M-60	Ikarus Blue Danube	C49Ft	Apr-91	Feb 92	Apr 95	ex Hills, Tredegar
29	F23 LBW	Volvo B10M-61	Ikarus Blue Danube	C49Ft	Feb 89	Mar 93	Apr 94	ex McLean's, Witney
30	F24 LBW	Volvo B10M-61	Ikarus Blue Danube	C49Ft	Feb 89	Mar 93	Apr 94	ex McLean's, Witney
31	F337 CHE	Volvo B10M-60	Ikarus Blue Danube	C49Ft	Aug 88	Mar 93	Apr 94	ex McLean's, Witney
3	L210 GJO	Volvo B10M-60	Jonckheere Deauville 45	C49Ft	Aug 93	Aug 93	Jan 98	
4	L211 GJO	Volvo B10M-60	Jonckheere Deauville 45	C49Ft	Aug 93	Aug 93	Jan 98	
5	L212 GJO	Volvo B10M-60	Jonckheere Deauville 45	C49Ft	Aug 93	Aug 93	Jan 98	
6	L213 GJO	Volvo B10M-60	Jonckheere Deauville 45	C49Ft	Aug 93	Aug 93	1997	
7	L214 GJO	Volvo B10M-60	Jonckheere Deauville 45	C49Ft	Aug-93	Aug 93	Jan 98	
1	L723 JUD	Volvo B10M-60	Jonckheere Deauville 45	C49Ft	Jan 94	Jan 94	May 99	
2	L724 JUD	Volvo B10M-60	Jonckheere Deauville 45	C49Ft	Jan 94	Jan 94	May 99	
18	L155 LBW	Volvo B10M-62	Jonckheere Deauville 45	C49Ft	Apr 94	Apr 94	1999	
29	L156 LBW	Volvo B10M-62	Jonckheere Deauville 45	C49Ft	Apr 94	Apr 94	1999	
30	L157 LBW	Volvo B10M-62	Jonckheere Deauville 45	C49Ft	Apr 94	Apr 94	1999	
31	L158 LBW	Volvo B10M-62	Jonckheere Deauville 45	C49Ft	Apr 94	Apr 94	1999	
21	L159 LBW	Volvo B10M-62	Jonckheere Deauville 45	C49Ft	Apr 94	Apr 94	May 99	
10	H639 UWR	Volvo B10M-60	Plaxton Paramount III 3500	C48Ft	Mar 91	Oct 94	1999	ex Wallace Arnold, Leeds
11	H640 UWR	Volvo B10M-60	Plaxton Paramount III 3500	C48Ft	Mar 91	Oct 94	1999	ex Wallace Arnold, Leeds
15	H641 UWR	Volvo B10M-60	Plaxton Paramount III 3500	C48Ft	Mar 91	Oct 94	1999	ex Wallace Arnold, Leeds
17	H650 UWR	Volvo B10M-60	Plaxton Paramount III 3500	C48Ft	Mar 91	Nov 94	1999	ex Wallace Arnold, Leeds
9	M103 XBW	Volvo B10M-62	Berkhof Excellence 1000LD	C51Ft	Apr 95	Apr 95	Sep 99	
16	M104 XBW	Volvo B10M-62	Berkhof Excellence 1000LD	C51Ft	Apr 95	Apr 95	1999	
25	M105 XBW	Volvo B10M-62	Berkhof Excellence 1000LD	C51Ft	Apr 95	Apr 95	1999	
26	M106 XBW	Volvo B10M-62	Berkhof Excellence 1000LD	C51Ft	Apr 95	Apr -95	1999	
28	M107 XBW	Volvo B10M-62	Berkhof Excellence 1000LD	C51Ft	Apr 95	Apr 95	1999	
8	N41 MJO	Volvo B10M-62	Berkhof Excellence 1000LD	C51Ft	Apr 96	Apr 96	May 99	
12	N42 MJO	Volvo B10M-62	Berkhof Excellence 1000LD	C51Ft	Apr 96	Apr 96	May 99	
14	N43 MJO	Volvo B10M-62	Berkhof Excellence 1000LD	C51Ft	Apr 96	Apr 96	May 99	
19	N45 MJO	Volvo B10M-62	Berkhof Excellence 1000LD	C51Ft	Apr 96	Apr 96	May 99	
23	N46 MJO	Volvo B10M-62	Berkhof Excellence 1000LD	C51Ft	Apr 96	Apr 96	May 99	
32	N47 MJO	Volvo B10M-62	Berkhof Excellence 1000LD	C51Ft	Apr 96	Apr 96	May 99	
33	N48 MJO	Volvo B10M-62	Berkhof Excellence 1000LD	C51Ft	Apr 96	Apr 96	May 99	
3	3063 VC	Volvo B10M-60	Plaxton Paramount III 3500	C48Ft	Mar 90	1997	Apr 99	ex Stagecoach Midland Red (66); new to Wallace Arnold, Paignton, as G543 LWU
6	9258 VC	Volvo B10M-60	Plaxton Paramount III 3500	C48Ft	Mar 90	1997	May 99	ex Stagecoach Midland Red (67); new to Wallace Arnold, Paignton, as G554 LWU
22	J456 FSR	Volvo B10M-61	Plaxton Expressliner	C46Ft	Mar 92	1997	1999	ex Stagecoach Midland Red (21); new to Express Travel Services, Perth (456)
20	J420 HDS	Volvo B10M-60	Plaxton Excalibur	C44Ft	Mar 92	Sep 97	1999	ex Stagecoach Busways (85); new to Park's, Hamilton
24	J424 HDS	Volvo B10M-60	Plaxton Excalibur	C44Ft	Mar 92	Sep 97	1998	ex Stagecoach Busways (87); new to Park's, Hamilton
(500)34	T34 DFC	MAN 24.350	Jonckheere Monaco	CH53/15Dt	May 99	May 99	2004	
(500)35	T35 DFC	MAN 24.350	Jonckheere Monaco	CH53/15Dt	Apr 99	Apr 99	2004	
(500)36	T36 DFC	MAN 24.350	Jonckheere Monaco	CH53/15Dt	Mar 99	Mar 99	2004	
(500)37	T37 BBW	MAN 24.350	Jonckheere Monaco	CH53/15Dt	May 99	May 99	2004	
(500)38	T38 BBW	MAN 24.350	Jonckheere Monaco	CH53/15Dt	May 99	May 99	2004	
(500)39	T39 BBW	MAN 24.350	Jonckheere Monaco	CH53/15Dt	May 99	May 99	2004	
(500)40 †	T40 UBE	MAN 24.350	Jonckheere Monaco	CH53/15Dt	May 99	May 99	2004	
(500)41	T41 BBW	MAN 24.350	Jonckheere Monaco	CH53/15Dt	May 99	May 99	2004	
(500)42	T42 BBW	MAN 24.350	Jonckheere Monaco	CH53/15Dt	May 99	May 99	2004	
(500)43	T43 BBW	MAN 24.350	Jonckheere Monaco	CH53/15Dt	Jun 99	Jun 99	2004	
(500)44	T44 UBE	MAN 24.350	Jonckheere Monaco	CH53/15Dt	Jul 99	Jul 99	2004	
(500)45	T45 BBW	MAN 24.350	Jonckheere Monaco	CH53/15Dt	Jun 99	Jun 99	2004	
(500)46 †	T46 BBW	MAN 24.350	Jonckheere Monaco	CH53/15Dt	May 99	May 99	2004	
(500)47 †	T47 BBW	MAN 24.350	Jonckheere Monaco	CH53/15Dt	May 99	May 99	2004	
(500)48	T48 BBW	MAN 24.350	Jonckheere Monaco	CH53/15Dt	May 99	May 99	2004	
(500)49	T49 BBW	MAN 24.350	Jonckheere Monaco	CH53/15Dt	May 99	May 99	2004	
(500)50	T50 UBE	MAN 24.350	Jonckheere Monaco	CH53/15Dt	Jun 99	Jun 99	2004	

No	Registration	Chassis	Body	Seats	New	In	Out	Notes
(500)51	T51 BBW	MAN 24.350	Jonckheere Monaco	CH53/15Dt	May 99	May 99	2004	
(500)52	T52 BBW	MAN 24.350	Jonckheere Monaco	CH53/15Dt	Jul 99	Jul 99	2004	
(500)53	T53 BBW	MAN 24.350	Jonckheere Monaco	CH53/15Dt	Jun 99	Jun 99	2004	
(500)54	T54 BBW	MAN 24.350	Jonckheere Monaco	CH53/15Dt	Jun 99	Jun 99	2004	
(500)55	T55 UBE	MAN 24.350	Jonckheere Monaco	CH53/15Dt	Jul 99	Jul 99	2004	
(500)56	T56 BBW	MAN 24.350	Jonckheere Monaco	CH53/15Dt	Aug 99	Aug 99	2004	
(500)57	T57 BBW	MAN 24.350	Jonckheere Monaco	CH53/15Dt	Jul 99	Jul 99	2004	
(500)58 †	T58 BBW	MAN 24.350	Jonckheere Monaco	CH53/15Dt	Jul 99	Jul 99	2004	
(500)59	T59 BBW	MAN 24.350	Jonckheere Monaco	CH53/15Dt	Aug 99	Aug 99	2004	
(500)60	T60 UBE	MAN 24.350	Jonckheere Monaco	CH53/15Dt	Jul 99	Jul 99	2004	
(500)66	W66 BBW	MAN 24.350	Jonckheere Monaco	CH53/15Dt	Jul 00	Jul 00	2004	
50101	KP04 GJE	Neoplan Skyliner N122/3L		CH63/18Dt	Jul 04	Jul 04	2009	
50102	KP04 GJF	Neoplan Skyliner N122/3L		CH63/18Dt	Jul 04	Jul 04	2009	
50103	KP04 GJG	Neoplan Skyliner N122/3L		CH63/18Dt	Jul 04	Jul 04	2009	
50104	KP04 GJJ	Neoplan Skyliner N122/3L		CH63/18Dt	Jul 04	Jul 04	2009	
50105	KP04 GJK	Neoplan Skyliner N122/3L		CH63/18Dt	Jul 04	Jul 04	2009	
50106	KP04 GJU	Neoplan Skyliner N122/3L		CH63/18Dt	Jul 04	Jul 04	2009	
50107	KP04 GJV	Neoplan Skyliner N122/3L		CH63/18Dt	Jul 04	Jul 04	2009	
50108	KP04 GJX	Neoplan Skyliner N122/3L		CH63/18Dt	Jul 04	Jul 04	2009	
50109	KP04 GJY	Neoplan Skyliner N122/3L		CH63/18Dt	Jul 04	Jul 04	2009	
50110	KP04 GJZ	Neoplan Skyliner N122/3L		CH63/18Dt	Jul 04	Jul 04	2009	
50111	KP04 GKA	Neoplan Skyliner N122/3L		CH63/18Dt	Jul 04	Jul 04	2009	
50112	KP04 GKC	Neoplan Skyliner N122/3L		CH63/18Dt	Jul 04	Jul 04	2009	
50113	KP04 GKD	Neoplan Skyliner N122/3L		CH63/18Dt	Jul 04	Jul 04	2009	
50114	KP04 GKE	Neoplan Skyliner N122/3L		CH63/18Dt	Jul 04	Jul 04	2009	
50115	KP04 GKF	Neoplan Skyliner N122/3L		CH63/18Dt	Jul 04	Jul 04	2009	
50116	KP04 GKG	Neoplan Skyliner N122/3L		CH63/18Dt	Jul 04	Jul 04	2009	
50117	KP04 GKJ	Neoplan Skyliner N122/3L		CH63/18Dt	Jul 04	Jul 04	2009	
50118	KP04 GKK	Neoplan Skyliner N122/3L		CH63/18Dt	Jul 04	Jul 04	2009	
50119	KP04 GKL	Neoplan Skyliner N122/3L		CH63/18Dt	Jul 04	Jul 04	2009	
50120	KP04 GKN	Neoplan Skyliner N122/3L		CH63/18Dt	Aug 04	Aug 04	2009	
50121	T40 UBE	Neoplan Skyliner N122/3L		CH63/18Dt	Aug 04	Aug 04	2009	
50122	T44 UBE	Neoplan Skyliner N122/3L		CH63/18Dt	Aug 04	Aug 04	2009	
50123	T50 UBE	Neoplan Skyliner N122/3L		CH63/18Dt	Aug 04	Aug 04	2009	
50124	T55 UBE	Neoplan Skyliner N122/3L		CH63/18Dt	Aug 04	Aug 04	2009	
50125	T60 UBE	Neoplan Skyliner N122/3L		CH63/18Dt	Aug 04	Aug 04	2009	
50201	T40 UBE	Van Hool Astromega TD927		CH63/24Dt	Aug 09	Aug 09	current	
50202	T44 UBE	Van Hool Astromega TD927		CH63/24Dt	Jul 09	Jul 09	current	
50203	T50 UBE	Van Hool Astromega TD927		CH63/24Dt	Jul 09	Jul 09	current	
50204	T55 UBE	Van Hool Astromega TD927		CH63/24Dt	Jul 09	Jul 09	current	
50205	T60 UBE	Van Hool Astromega TD927		CH63/24Dt	Jul 09	Jul 09	current	
50206	OU09 FMY	Van Hool Astromega TD927		CH63/24Dt	Jul 09	Jul 09	current	
50207	OU09 FMZ	Van Hool Astromega TD927		CH63/24Dt	Jul 09	Jul 09	current	
50208	OU09 FMA	Van Hool Astromega TD927		CH63/24Dt	Jul 09	Jul 09	current	
50209	OU09 FNC	Van Hool Astromega TD927		CH63/24Dt	Jul 09	Jul 09	current	
50210	OU09 FND	Van Hool Astromega TD927		CH63/24Dt	Jul 09	Jul 09	current	
50211	OU09 FNE	Van Hool Astromega TD927		CH63/24Dt	Aug 09	Aug 09	current	
50212	OU09 FNF	Van Hool Astromega TD927		CH63/24Dt	Jul 09	Jul 09	current	
50213	OU09 FNG	Van Hool Astromega TD927		CH63/24Dt	Aug 09	Aug 09	current	
50214	OU09 FNH	Van Hool Astromega TD927		CH63/24Dt	Aug 09	Aug 09	current	
50215	OU09 FNJ	Van Hool Astromega TD927		CH63/24Dt	Aug 09	Aug 09	current	
50216	OU59 AVC	Van Hool Astromega TD927		CH63/24Dt	Sep 09	Sep 09	current	
50217	OU59 AVD	Van Hool Astromega TD927		CH63/24Dt	Sep 09	Sep 09	current	
50218	OU59 AVE	Van Hool Astromega TD927		CH63/24Dt	Sep 09	Sep 09	current	
50219	OU59 AUR	Van Hool Astromega TD927		CH63/24Dt	Sep 09	Sep 09	current	
50220	OU59 AUO	Van Hool Astromega TD927		CH63/24Dt	Sep 09	Sep 09	current	
50221	OU59 AUT	Van Hool Astromega TD927		CH63/24Dt	Sep 09	Sep 09	current	
50222	OU59 AUV	Van Hool Astromega TD927		CH63/24Dt	Sep 09	Sep 09	current	
50223	OU59 AUW	Van Hool Astromega TD927		CH63/24Dt	Sep 09	Sep 09	current	
50224	OU59 AUX	Van Hool Astromega TD927		CH63/24Dt	Sep 09	Sep 09	current	
50225	OU59 AUY	Van Hool Astromega TD927		CH63/24Dt	Sep 09	Sep 09	current	
50226	OU59 AVB	Van Hool Astromega TD927		CH63/24Dt	Sep 09	Sep 09	current	

No	Registration	Chassis	Body	Seats	New	In	Out	Notes
On loan:								
	J426 HDS	Volvo B10M-60	Plaxton Excalibur	C44Ft	Mar 92	Nov 93	Jan 94	from Park's, Hamilton
	J429 HDS	Volvo B10M-60	Plaxton Excalibur	C44Ft	Apr 92	Dec 93	Jan 94	from Park's, Hamilton
	N561 SJF	Volvo B10MA-55	Jonckheere Mistral 35	AC72F	Jun 96	Aug 97	Aug 97	from Stagecoach Fife Scottish (561)
	M332 GFW	Volvo B10M-62	Caetano Algarve II	C49Ft	Apr 95	Nov 98	1999	from Dawson Rentals; new to Daisy Bus Service, Broughton
	P186 NAK	Volvo B10M-62	Plaxton Première 350	C49Ft	Apr 97	Nov 98	1999	from Kirby Leasing; new to Kilpatrick, Glenrothes
	4828 VC	Leyland Tiger TRCTL11//3RH	Plaxton Paramount II 3500LS	C51Ft	Aug 85	Nov 98	Jan 99	from Stagecoach Midland Red (74)
	9737 VC	Leyland Tiger TRCTL11//3RH	Plaxton Paramount II 3500LS	C51Ft	Sep 85	Dec 98	Feb 99	from Stagecoach Midland Red (75)
13646	H463 EJR	Leyland Olympian ON3R49C18Z4	Alexander RH	DPH53/41F	Jan 91	Jul 06	Aug 06	from Stagecoach South (13646)
13652	H462 EJR	Leyland Olympian ON3R49C18Z4	Alexander RH	DPH53/41F	Feb 91	Jul 06	Aug 06	from Stagecoach South (13652)
50133	CN05 APV	Neoplan Skyliner N122/3L		CH63/18Dt	Mar 05	Aug 08	Aug 09	from Stagecoach Western Buses (50133)

*   returned on loan from Yeates, Loughborough (dealer), in June 1994
†   returned on loan from Megabus in 2005

Above: **Jonckheere Modulo-bodied MAN 24.350 No 40 (T40 UBE) pulls out of George Street, Oxford as it begins another run to the capital.** MALCOLM CROWE

Appendix 3: Mega-rears

The impressive rear-end branding applied to the Van Hool Astromega fleet sends a very clear message to people following the coaches, brightening up what might otherwise be a dull day.
The table below is included courtesy of Rob Williams.

50201	Burn it at Both Ends
50202	Burn it at Both Ends
50203	The West End
50204	Oxford … the City Inspires
50205	The Big Smoke Without the Smoke
50206	The Capital for less Capital
50207	Business Coaching
50208	The West End
50209	The West End
50210	Business Coaching
50211	Westfield Shopping Centre
50212	Westfield Shopping Centre
50213	Oxford … the City Inspires
50214	The Big Smoke without the Smoke
50215	The Capital for less Capital
50216	Oxford … the City Inspires
50217	Oxford … the City Inspires

50218	Business Coaching
50219	Westfield Shopping Centre
50220	Westfield Shopping Centre
50221	The Big Smoke Without the Smoke
50222	Burn it at Both Ends
50223	The Capital for less Capital
50224	The Capital for less Capital
50225	The Big Smoke Without the Smoke
50226	Business Coaching

Appendix 4: Literature

A selection of publicity material used by the Oxford Tube.

Appendix 5: Logos

Logos used by the Oxford Tube and Megabus.

Appendix 6:
Megabus today

As this book is written at the beginning of 2012 Megabus is going from strength to strength and now serves nearly 100 destinations throughout the UK, as well as Rosslare in the Republic of Ireland. Many services are run by 15m Plaxton-bodied Volvo B12B tri-axle coaches, while Van Hool Astromegas provide additional capacity on busy routes, often pulling the trailers first seen in use with their predecessors, the Neoplan Skyliners.

The latest initiative involves a sleeper-coach service from London to Glasgow, which started in October 2011, using articulated coaches, and further exciting new developments are in the planning stage.

With the exception of the Oxford service, all services now use Victoria Coach Station — a sure sign that Megabus has come of age.

Above: **Stagecoach Warwickshire took delivery of this Plaxton Panther 2-bodied Volvo B9R in 2011. No 53645 (KX61 GFE) typifies Megabus deliveries at the time of writing.** MALCOLM CROWE

Below: **Vehicles concurrently being delivered included a considerable number of Van Hool Astromegas similar to those used on the Oxford Tube. No 50233 (CN61 FAA) of Stagecoach in South Wales sets out from Victoria for Cardiff.** MALCOLM CROWE